The Butterfield Overland Mail Route Through Southern California 1858-1861

©2013 Kirby Sanders

- First edition April, 2013 -

Published by the author via Amazon CreateSpace
ISBN: 1484057228
ISBN 13: 978-1484057223

ii

ACKNOWLEDGEMENTS

Particular thanks are due to Mr. Frank Norris and Mr. Aaron Mahr for shepherding me through the National Park Service processes and protocols. A second round of thanks to Mr. Norris for his technical editing assistance and erudite questions for clarification in the preparation of the reports. The numbers of individual local researchers who assisted by answering questions about their specific areas are too numerous to mention. However, special notice and thanks are due to authors Gerald Ahnert and George Hackler as well as researchers Don & Paul Matt, Fred Yeck, Chris Wray and other members of the Oregon-California Trails Association and the Santa Clarita Valley (CA) Historical Society. Also many thanks to my Arkansas trail buddy Scott Mashburn and to Marilyn Heifner, John McLarty, Glenn Jones and all of the members of the Heritage Trail Partners organization in Northwest Arkansas. Note to Glenn – "never trust a man with a ponytail."

CONTENTS

Author's Foreword ~ How To Use This Book   1

1   Introduction and Historical Background   2

2   Swiveller's Ranch (Arizona) to Fort Yuma (California)   19

3   Fort Yuma to Pilot Knob Mcsa   26

4   Pilot Knob Mesa to Indian Wells   31

5   Indian Wells to Carrizo Creek Station   38

6   Carrizo Creek Station to Palm Springs Station   43

7   Palm Springs Station to Vallecito Station   47

8   Vallecito Station to San Felipe Station   51

9   San Felipe Station to Warner Ranch   56

10 Warner Ranch to Oak Grove Station   60

11 Oak Grove Station to Aguanga, California   64

12 Aguanga, California, to Temecula, California   69

13 Temecula, California, to Laguna Grande   75

14 Laguna Grande to Rancho Temescal   80

15 Rancho Temescal to Rancho Chino   85

16 Rancho Chino to San Jose, California   91

17 San Jose, California to El Monte, California   99

18 El Monte, California to Los Angeles   103

19 Los Angeles to Campo de Cahuenga   107

20 Campo de Cahuenga to Mission San Fernando Rey   112

21 Mission San Fernando Rey to Hart's Station   116

22 Hart's Station to King's Station   121

23 King's Station to Widow Smith's Station   126

24 Widow Smith's Station to French John's Station   131

25 French John's Station to Reed's Ranch   137

26 Reed's Ranch to Fort Tejon   142

AUTHOR'S FOREWORD ~ HOW TO USE THIS BOOK

During 2010 and 2011, I was selected and tasked by the U.S. National Park Service (NPS) to prepare a preliminary series of reports and maps delineating the routes and known or presumed station locations used by the Butterfield Overland Mail Company for the first overland transcontinental mail service in American history. Said reports were to be included in an overall Special Resource Study to determine the eligibility of and potential for establishing the Butterfield route as a recognized National Trail under the administration and jurisdiction of NPS. The overall study and my portion thereof were mandated by order of Congress and signed into law by President Barack Obama under auspices of the Omnibus Public Lands Act of 2009.

The result of this work was eight hundred eighty-nine (889) pages of reports and documentation along with one hundred seventy-five (175) accompanying maps. What follows here are the resulting documents as filed with the NPS. The work was to be a bibliographic study to establish the routes and stations as nearly as possible given existing research. It is hoped that the National Trail designation will be approved and that future additional research on the ground will result in a final and specific understanding and mapping of the entire route.

Given the volume of the reports, I have broken them out into several books that will cover the seven states involved in the study -- Missouri, Arkansas, Oklahoma, Texas, New Mexico, Arizona and California. This volume will cover the route from Swiveller's Station in Arizona through to Fort Tejon. The balance of California is included in a separate volume.

It should also be noted that in some cases, additional details have been discovered since the close of the NPS study period that have helped pin down or more accurately point toward certain station locations that had remained obscure. The effected reports have been annotated to update the most current information available as of this writing.

The maps contained in these reports were generated on a Google Maps base. Blue lines on maps indicate modern driving routes while red lines indicate the probable actual routes. Red lines only indicate the modern driving route approximates the actual route. Multi-colored lines indicate the likelihood of several different routes having been used at various times through the operation of the Butterfield stagecoaches. A digital database of the maps in this book has also been generated. The database maps contain driving directions for the recommended modern routes. For permission to access that database, contact the author via email at kirby.sanders.biz@gmail.com and an html format index including all seven states in the study will be provided.

Dates on the individual reports denote the date the report was prepared for submission to NPS. It should also be noted that these reports were intended as specific field-guide notes rather than for entertainment.

INTRODUCTION AND HISTORICAL BACKGROUND
The Butterfield Overland Mail Ox-Bow Route
1858 - 1861
Prepared by Kirby Sanders for National Park Service
February 14, 2011

Purpose:

The purpose of this overall study is to establish a preliminary overview of the route and stations of the Butterfield Overland Mail Ox Bow Route (1858-1861) for use in preparation of the National Park Service Special Resource Study for the proposed Butterfield Overland Mail Ox Bow Route National Trail as mandated in Subtitle C; Section 7211 of the Omnibus Public Land Management Act of 2009 (Public Law 111-11).

Historical Significance:

The Butterfield Overland Mail Ox-Bow Route, for all that it was short-lived, has a well-deserved historical position behind its iconic stature in the lore of the American West and the popular culture that arose around it.

United States Territorial Acquisitions 1803 - 1853

The Butterfield Overland Mail represents a bold and important step toward unifying the United States as a nation whose territory had only recently spread "from sea to shining sea."

The Louisiana Purchase of 1803 brought 828,800 square miles of what is now the American Heartland into possession of the United States.

The annexation of the Republic of Texas in 1845 brought what is now the Lone Star State -- as well as parts of Colorado, Kansas, New Mexico, Oklahoma, and Wyoming.

By 1846, the relinquishment of the British to claims on the Oregon Territory filled in the Northwestern corner of the continental United States territory.

The Mexican Cession of California in 1848 pushed the boundary of the United States' lands south along the balance of the Pacific Coast and solidified the hold on the western and northern segments of the Texas claim.

Establishment of the Minnesota Territory in 1849 solidified the northern portion of the "Heartland." The Gadsden Purchase of 1853 filled in the last "piece of the puzzle" by establishing the definitive southern border of U.S. territory along the Rio Grande River in New Mexico and Arizona.

By the middle 1850s, the territory of the United States of America had expanded to what we now recognize as the "Continental U.S.", but it was hardly the coalition of states we recognize today. The State of Texas was recognized in its current form as of 1845. By 1850, what we now recognize as California had achieved statehood -- but much of the Intermountain West remained territorial -- sparsely settled and without the national representation that came with statehood.

"31 Star" Flag of the United States 1851 – 1858

By 1857 the midsection of the country was a gulf of territories separating the State of California from the other states.

Sixteen of what we now recognize as the "lower 48" states were territories rather than fully vested states. The present-day states of Minnesota, North Dakota, South Dakota, Nebraska, Kansas, Oklahoma, New Mexico, Colorado, Wyoming, Montana, Idaho, Utah, Arizona, Nevada, Oregon and Washington were all territories rather than fully vested states.

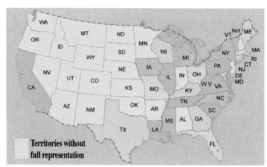

States and Territories of the United States as of 1857

Despite the territorial acquisitions that created a legitimate Continental United States, the 31 States and intervening Territories were not a nation that could readily communicate "from sea to shining sea".

Sending a simple letter or newspaper from New York to San Francisco during the mid-1850s could be accomplished one of three ways:
  • by ship around the bottom of South America at Tierra Fuego,
  • by ship to Panama for a (not always reliable) overland passage across the isthmus and north again by steamship, or
  • by ship or riverboat to New Orleans for another ship's passage along the northern fringe of the Gulf of Mexico to Indianola TX for an overland journey to San Diego -- and another ship's passage onward to reach to San Francisco.

At best, one could expect one's letter or newspaper to arrive at its destination -- if it arrived at all -- within three months or so.

Socio-politically, by the mid-1850s, the "western states" (everything west of the Mississippi River -- Iowa, Missouri, Arkansas, Texas and California) as well as the southwestern territories were feeling "disconnected" as Americans. They were part of "one great nation" -- but could not easily get mail to or from family in the various eastern states. Meanwhile, rumblings in "the South" began to echo feelings of disenfranchisement as well -- but with far more dire talk of possible repercussions.

The 34th United States Congress responded with the passage of a postal act that required overland mail delivery by rail and coach between St. Louis MO and San Francisco CA via "the best valleys and passages" within 25 days -- which service should also accommodate passengers. That act also required that a reliable overland mail route connect the southern states to the west and southwest via Memphis TN.

Supporters of the project such as Senators William M. Gwin and John B. Weller (California) and Thomas J. Rusk (Texas) argued that their states and the territories deserved adequate mail service and that such service would help to spur settlement and economic development in the territories.

Opponents generally argued that the Post Office should be self-supporting and that establishing the overland route would be too expensive to implement and had no promise of unsubsidized economic viability. Additionally, many of the Southern Senators felt the new service would favor the northern states with inadequate benefit to the South.

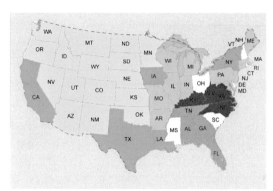

34th Senate vote on the 1857 Overland Mail Appropriation Bill

In February of 1857, the Senate approved the general plan for an overland mail service with a 24 - 10 vote as follows:
  • California, Texas, Louisiana, Iowa, New York (two yea votes each)
  • Arkansas, Missouri, Illinois, Wisconsin, Indiana, Michigan, Pennsylvania, Maryland, New Jersey, Connecticut, Massachusetts, Maine (one yea vote, one not voting)
  • Kentucky, Virginia, North Carolina (two nay votes)
  • Tennessee, Alabama, Georgia, Florida (one nay vote, one not voting)
  • Mississippi, South Carolina, Ohio, Delaware, Rhode Island, New Hampshire (neither Senator voted).
It is interesting to note that none of the states split with a one yea / one nay vote.

The House of Representatives, however, did not pass the postal appropriation-- instead sending the bill to joint committee for further amendment. A House / Senate compromise bill was eventually approved and the basic Overland Mail bill was passed in September of 1857.

Enter John Butterfield and the Overland Mail Company. Butterfield was a successful (and politically well-connected) stagecoach and freight operator in New York and founder of the American Express Company. In conjunction with western partners Henry Wells and William G. Fargo (Wells Fargo Company), the Overland Mail Company was formed in 1857 and registered three of the nine operating proposals that were filed with Postmaster General Aaron V. Brown (a former governor of Tennessee).

Brown required that the Overland Mail Route be established "from St. Louis, Missouri, and from Memphis, Tennessee, converging at Little Rock,

Arkansas; thence via Preston, Texas, or as nearly so as may be found advisable, to the best point of crossing the Rio Grande above El Paso and not far from Fort Fillmore (NM); thence, along the new road being opened and constructed under the direction of the Secretary of the Interior, to Fort Yuma, California; thence through the best passes and along the best valleys for safe and expeditious staging, to San Francisco."

On September 16, 1857 the Overland Mail Company was awarded a six year contract for operation of the postal route with service to begin in September 1858.

While none of the bids followed his route exactly, Postmaster General Brown selected one of the three Butterfield proposals with agreement that the basic route outline be followed with latitude for minor revisions on Butterfield's part in the interests of "safety, speed of mail and passenger delivery and reliability of roads." It is important to note, given this agreement, that the final Butterfield Overland Route from Memphis bypassed both Little Rock AR and Preston TX.

It is also important to note that the establishment of the Memphis to Ft. Smith route placated some of the southern objections by assuring the southern states that they would have convenient service -- although the people of Little Rock AR were never happy with the fact that they were bypassed. That bypass is a point of historical controversy to this day.

Initially, Little Rock was identified as an important potential hub at the convergence of the two routes originating from Saint Louis and Memphis. Unfortunately for Little Rock, the swampy terrain between Memphis and Little Rock barred a functional overland road between the two cities, erratic water levels on the connecting watercourses made steamboat traffic unreliable and the failure of the Memphis - Little Rock Railroad to complete through tracks between the two cities rendered an unworkable route by any conveyance from Memphis to Little Rock.

Butterfield effected a "fix" to this problem by following ground and ridge lines along the 1830s Military Road and continued well to the north of Little Rock. This shift along the Memphis - West road established the convergence of the two legs of the Butterfield Route at Fort Smith AR rather than Little Rock.

Thus the route was fixed -- traveling through the States (and Territories) of Missouri, Arkansas, Oklahoma, Texas, New Mexico, Arizona and California.

Establishing the Butterfield Route in Modern Terms

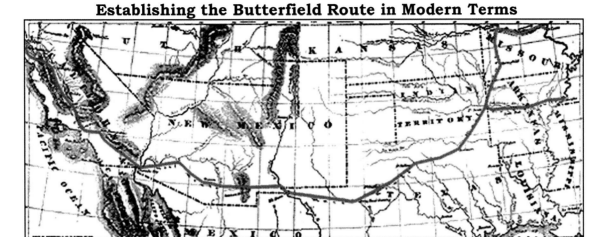

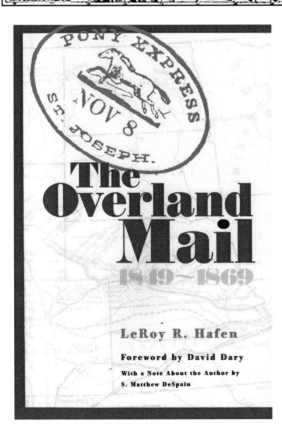

For historical background and sociopolitical overview, there are two primary studies that must be considered -- Leroy R. Hafen's *The Overland Mail, 1849-1869: Promoter of Settlement, Precursor of Railroads* (original publication by A. H. Clarke Company, 1926; Cleveland OH; Republished by University of Oklahoma Press; Norman OK, 2004) and Walter B. Lang's volumes *The First Overland Main Butterfield Trail St. Louis to San Francisco 1858-1861* and *The First Overland Mail, Butterfield Trail, San Francisco to Memphis, 1858-1861* (published by Roycrofters; East Aurora, New York, 1945).

Hafen is an excellent analysis of the sociopolitical background. Lang's work consists mainly of collected contemporaneous travelers' journals and news articles and is more valuable as a resource for the preparation of interpretive materials than for route identification.

Establishing the Butterfield Route in modern terms is not without some challenges as no other effort to track the entire route has been attempted for several decades. Much of the bibliographic data outlining the Butterfield Route is either out-of-date in terms of modern roads and / or out-of-print.

There are two primary contemporary reports that recount the entire Butterfield route in 1858. The first of those is the account of Waterman L. Ormsby. Ormsby was correspondent for the *New York Herald* newspaper who traveled the entire Butterfield route on its first westbound trip in 1858 and filed dispatches published in *the Herald*.

The second is a report by Goddard Bailey, a postal inspector who made the first eastbound trip and reported the point-to-point mileage between stations to Postmaster General Aaron V. Brown.

Ormsby's account mentions several identifiable landmarks along the route (although he does not specifically mention all of the stations) while Bailey gives an exact inventory of the stations and the miles between them.

Ormsby's account has been published and remains in-print (*The Butterfield Overland Mail - Only Through Passenger on the First Westbound Stage*; original publications New York Herald (NY) Sep 26 - Nov 19, 1858; republished by Henry E. Huntington Library and Art Gallery, San Marino CA, 1942 - 1998).

Bailey's itinerary was widely published in newspapers at the time (including the *New York Times*). His full report was also published in *De Bow's Review and Industrial Resources, Statistics etc*; (New Orleans and Washington City; 1858).

During the 1930s, Roscoe P. and Margaret B. Conkling used the Bailey and Ormsby data to plot and travel the 1858 Butterfield Route and documented several later station locations (1859-1861) as well.

Their research is now out-of-print, but was published (*The Butterfield Overland Mail,1857–1869*; Three Volumes; Glendale, CA: A. H. Clark Company, 1947.) Full three-volume sets are now hard to come by and generally very expensive when they can be found.

The Conklings' research became the foundational resource for many subsequent Butterfield research efforts.

Unfortunately, however, many of the roads traveled by the Conklings in the 1930s have also become difficult (if not impossible) to discover -- rendering it often difficult to translate their route descriptions into modern terms.

Additionally, as local historians, later scholars and agencies have tracked the Butterfield Route in the ensuing years; some have faulted the Conklings' accuracy and methodology. The most frequent criticism in situations where additional findings do not mesh with the Conklings is that the Conklings relied on deductive processes to establish their routings and oral history interviews with site claimants as of the 1930s to establish station sites, but failed to adequately verify their conclusions and interviewees' statements to historical maps and records.

Throughout the preparation of this study, the Conklings have been used and cited as a foundational resource. Their dedication and years of work should be respected and honored, but not necessarily sanctified. For the purposes of this study, the Conklings have been considered to be a resource for equal consideration, but not the final word.

There was a national Butterfield Centennial recognition organized state-by-state in conjunction with the United States Post Office in 1958, however the information gathered by the State Committees does not appear to have been centralized. Additionally, records and reports from the state committees are sometimes difficult to come by and vary greatly in the amount of detail they contain. The records from the State of Oklahoma are well-detailed, excellent resources. The Arkansas report is rather brief and very general -- particularly regarding much of the Memphis to Ft. Smith Route.

It should be noted that the Missouri Butterfield Centennial Committee erected markers at each of the Butterfield Station locations in Missouri, most of which have been documented by Donald Mincke (*Chasing the Butterfield Overland Mail Stage -- A Road Guide Following the old Stage Route Across Missouri and Arkansas*). To date, however, no records of reports by that Committee or inventory of the markers have been located within the archives of the State Historical Society of Missouri.

To date, no archive of Centennial Committee reports have been located from the states of Texas, New Mexico, Arizona or California.

The National Coordinator of the 1958 Butterfield Centennial effort was one Vernon Brown of Tulsa OK. Archives of the National Postal Museum in Washington DC contain a telegram from President Dwight David Eisenhower recognizing Mr. Brown's efforts as coordinator and the Butterfield Centennial project overall. Once again, however, neither the Postal Museum nor the Oklahoma Historical Society are in possession of Mr. Brown's notes and papers. Neither are they aware of where such collection might be -- or even if such a collection exists.

After the 1958 Butterfield Centennial effort, study of the Butterfield Route "went fallow" on the national front. It fell to individual authors and local / regional historical preservation organizations, genealogical societies and museums to be the "keepers of the flame" for the Butterfield Route.

Methodology in Establishing the Butterfield Stations and Landmarks in Modern Terms

1] **[Sep. 16th, 1858.**

OVERLAND MAIL COMPANY.
THROUGH TIME SCHEDULE BETWEEN
ST. LOUIS, MO., MEMPHIS, TENN. } & SAN FRANCISCO, CAL.

GOING WEST.

LEAVE.	DAYS.	Hour.	Distance Place to Place	Time allowed.	Av'ge Miles per Hour.
St. Louis, Mo. & Memphis, Tenn. }	Every Monday & Thursday.	8.00 A.M	Miles.	No.Hours	
P. R. R. Terminus, "	" Monday & Thursday,	6.00 P.M	160	10	16
Springfield, "	" Wednesday & Saturday,	7.45 A.M	143	37¾	3¾
Fayetteville, "	" Thursday & Sunday,	10.15 A.M	100	26½	3¾
Fort Smith, Ark.	" Friday & Monday,	3.30 A.M	65	17¼	3¾
Sherman, Texas	" Sunday & Wednesday,	12.30 A.M	205	45	4½
Fort Belknap. "	" Monday & Thursday,	9.00 A.M	146½	32½	4½
Fort Chadbourn, "	" Tuesday & Friday,	3.15 P.M	136	30½	4½
Pecos River, (Em. Crossing)	" Thursday & Sunday,	3.45 A.M	165	36½	4½
El Paso,	" Saturday & Tuesday,	11.00 A.M	248½	55¼	4½
Soldier's Farewell	" Sunday & Wednesday,	8.30 P.M	150	33½	4½
Tucson, Arizona	" Tuesday & Friday,	1.30 P.M	184½	41	4½
Gila River," "	" Wednesday & Saturday,	9.00 P.M	141	31½	4½
Fort Yuma, Cal.	" Friday & Monday,	3.00 A.M	135	30	4½
San Bernardino "	" Saturday & Tuesday,	11.00 P.M	200	44	4½
Ft. Tejon, (Via Los Angeles)	" Monday & Thursday,	7.30 A.M	150	32½	4½
Visalia,	" Tuesday & Friday,	11.30 A.M	127	28	4½
Firebaugh's Ferry, "	" Wednesday & Saturday,	5.30 A.M	82	18	4½
(Arrive) San Francisco,	" Thursday & Sunday,	8.30 A.M	163	27	6

GOING EAST.

LEAVE.	DAYS.	Hour.	Distance Place to Place	Time allowed.	Av'ge Miles per Hour.
San Francisco, Cal.	Every Monday & Thursday,	8.00 A.M	Miles.	No.Hours	
Firebaugh's Ferry, "	" Tuesday & Friday,	11.00 A.M	163	27	6
Visalia,	" Wednesday & Saturday,	5.00 A.M	82	18	4½
Ft. Tejon, (Via Los Angeles)	" Thursday & Sunday,	9.00 A.M	127	28	4½
San Bernardino, "	" Friday & Monday,	5.30 P.M	150	32½	4½
Fort Yuma, "	" Sunday & Wednesday,	1.30 P.M	200	44	4½
Gila River," Arizona	" Monday & Thursday,	7.30 P.M	135	30	4½
Tucson, "	" Wednesday & Saturday	3.00 A.M	141	31½	4½
Soldier's Farewell,	" Thursday & Sunday,	8.00 P.M	184½	41	4½
El Paso, Tex.	" Saturday & Tuesday,	5.30 A.M	150	33½	4½
Pecos River, (Em. Crossing)	" Monday & Thursday	12.45 P.M	248½	55¼	4½
Fort Chadbourn, "	" Wednesday & Saturday	1.15 P.M	165	36½	4½
Fort Belknap, "	" Thursday & Sunday,	7.30 A.M	136	30½	4½
Sherman, "	" Friday & Monday,	4.00 P.M	146½	32½	4½
Fort Smith, Ark.	" Sunday & Wednesday,	1.00 P.M	205	45	4½
Fayetteville, Mo.	" Monday, & Thursday,	6.15 A.M	65	17¼	3¾
Springfield,	" Tuesday & Friday,	8.45 A.M	100	26½	3¾
P. R. R. Terminus, "	" Wednesday & Saturday	10.30 P.M	143	37¾	3¾
(Arrive) St. Louis, Mo. & Memphis, Tenn. }	" Thursday & Sunday,		160	10	16

This Schedule may not be exact—Superintendents, Agents, Station-men, Conductors, Drivers and all employees are particularly directed to use every possible exertion to get the Stages through in quick time, even though they may be ahead of this time.

If they are behind this time, it will be necessary to urge the animals on to the highest speed that they can be driven without injury.

Remember that no allowance is made in the time for ferries, changing teams, &c. It is therefore necessary that each driver increase his speed over the average per hour enough to gain the necessary time for meals, changing teams, crossing ferries, &c.

Every person in the Company's employ will always bear in mind that each minute of time is of importance. If each driver on the route loses fifteen (15) minutes, it would make a total loss of time, on the entire route, of twenty-five (25) hours, or, more than one day. If each one loses ten (10) minutes it would make a total loss of sixteen and one half (16½) hours, or, the best part of a day.

On the contrary, if each driver gains that amount of time, it leaves a margin of time against accidents and extra delays.

All hands will see the great necessity of promptness and dispatch; every minute of time is valuable as the Company are under heavy forfeit if the mail is behind time.

Conductors must note the hour and date of departure from Stations, the causes of delay, if any, and all particulars. They must also report the same fully to their respective Superintendents.

* The Station referred to is on Gila River, is 40 miles west of Maricopa Wells.

JOHN BUTTERFIELD.
Pres't.

Butterfield Schedule and Timetable as published by the Overland Mail Company, 1858

Many of the bibliographic resources that have been most helpful in locating the modern sites of the various Butterfield Stations are either privately published by the authors themselves, published by small and / or academic publishing houses or held in the archives of State Historical Societies or local museums. Of particular note for their modern regional or state research efforts are:

- Donald Mincke (Missouri and Arkansas)
- A.C. Greene (Texas)
- Don and Paul Matt (Missouri, Arkansas, Oklahoma and Texas)
- George Hackler (New Mexico)
- Gerald Ahnert (Arizona)
- Dan Talbot (Arizona)

In 2008, Casey Gill (curator of the Wells Fargo History Museum in San Diego CA) recreated the approximate route of the Butterfield from Saint Louis to San Francisco along modern roads in a recreational vehicle as part of the Wells Fargo Company's Butterfield Sesquicentennial recognition. Notes from his travels were posted to an Internet blog describing his journey.

Four of the regional offices of the Texas Heritage Trails Program have also been active in recent Butterfield Overland Mail research and should be more closely consulted for future Planning and Implementation / Interpretive projects. Those offices are the Lakes Trail Region located in Granbury, Fort Trail Region located in Abilene, the Pecos Trail Region located in Sonora, and the Mountain Trail Region located in Van Horn. The Lakes Trail Region has been particularly active in ongoing Butterfield Research.

The recent emergence of "geocaching" as a hobby has led to the establishment of numerous small Internet websites and "blogs" that contain helpful information regarding various Butterfield Station sites and related historical markers on the local level. With the modern availability of relatively inexpensive GPS devices, numerous local hobbyists have taken to logging the latitude and longitude coordinates of historical sites in their immediate neighborhoods on individual internet websites -- resulting in numerous widely scattered small resources for locating individual Butterfield-related sites.

The efforts of these amateur sleuths is commendable and should be taken into account -- although the quality of reporting is sometimes uneven.

Of particular merit in this arena is a website established by William Nienke and Sam Morrow in conjunction with the Texas Geocaching Association. That website contains a searchable database of latitude and longitude coordinates for most of the historical markers in Texas.

Of final note regarding the establishment of coordinates for Butterfield-related station sites, landmarks and relevant historical markers is the fact that many of the bibliographic resources (particularly those published in the 1930s through the 1950s) established the locations of the Butterfield Station sites by notation of Township, Range and Section description. In many cases, some of the more obscure station sites can be approximated in terms of latitude and longitude by converting and mapping the corners and centroid of those Township / Range / Section descriptions to determine approximate latitude and longitude coordinates for individual sites.

In some few cases, the actual station sites have been obscured (or obliterated) by time and progress. In those cases, the station locations have been approximated according to Bailey's mileages along the known route from the last known point, reputable modern research and (where they have been discovered) Civil War records. These obscured or approximated locations have been so noted in the narrative reports.

It should also be noted that there are occasional "spurious" reports of purported "Butterfield Stations" near (but not on) the documentable Butterfield Route. These cases do not seem to be malicious in intent. Generally they can be traced to post-contemporary diary entries that fail to take into account that the actual Butterfield Route may have been 20 or so miles distant -- and the actual stage that served a given community was a local or connecting trunk line operated by an independent carrier.

Granted -- there has come to be a certain romance to a "Butterfield connection," in the popular culture but in many cases these spurious claims appear to be a matter of misinterpretation of early diary entries.

Methodology in Establishing the Original Route in Modern Terms

The Overland Mail Company did not forge 3,000-plus miles of new trails and roads to establish their route as of 1858.

In mapping the approximate original Butterfield Route, contemporaneous route descriptions were compared to later field research (where available) -- always bearing In mind Postmaster General A.V. Brown's specific instructions in 1857:

> "from St. Louis, Missouri, and from Memphis, Tennessee, converging at Little Rock, Arkansas; thence via Preston, Texas, or as nearly so as may be found advisable, to the best point of crossing the Rio Grande above El Paso and not far from Fort Fillmore (NM); thence, along the new road being opened and constructed under the direction of the Secretary of the Interior, to Fort Yuma, California; thence through the best passes and along the best valleys for safe and expeditious staging, to San Francisco."

For the most part, the Butterfield Route connected several known roads -- in keeping with Postmaster Brown's instructions.

• In Missouri, the Butterfield Route originated by rail on the Pacific Railroad from St. Louis to Tipton MO and then Syracuse MO before tracking known local roads southward to Arkansas.

• Through western Arkansas, the route again tracked known local roads as well as those forged by the military in establishing the boundary with Indian Territory during the 1830s and 1840s as well as portions of the Trail of Tears routes used by the U.S. military during the Indian relocation movements of the 1830s. On the Memphis to Fort Smith leg, the Butterfield Route essentially tracks the Military Road established to link those two settlements in the late 1830s - early 1840s.

• Through Oklahoma and into Texas, The Butterfield Route followed documented Choctaw Nation roads established after the relocation of 1830 into the historic "Texas Road" / Osage Trace that was the main emigrant route and Military Road from Fort Gibson, Kansas to Texas predating the Butterfield.

• As a general reference, much of the Butterfield route roughly traced roads described by Randolph Barnes Marcy from Fort Smith AR to Dona Ana NM in the 1840s (published as *The Prairie Traveler - A Handbook for Overland Expeditions*; New York; Harper & Brothers; 1859).

• In Northeast and North Central Texas, the Butterfield route diverged from Marcy's 1849 expedition route but appears to roughly track other trails identified by Marcy during another expedition through Texas in 1854.

• Through western New Mexico and Arizona, the Butterfield Route tracks routes identified by John Russell Bartlett (1850-1853) during his survey as Boundary Commissioner to establish the U.S. / Mexico border in conjunction with negotiation of the Gadsden Purchase (published in *Personal Narrative of Explorations and Incidents in Texas, New Mexico, California, Sonora and Chihuahua*; D. Appleton and Company; New York; 1854). This route also follows sections of the Mormon Battalion route from Kanesville (Council Bluffs) IA to San Diego CA (1846-1847).

• In western Arizona and into Southern California, the Butterfield Route substantially tracked the early route of the Juan Bautista de Anza expedition (1774), as did Bartlett.

• Into Central and Northern California, the Butterfield Route roughly tracks the de Anza (with some modifications) as well as the Camino Real / Mission Trail (1600s) and several local trails that connected gold camps and settlements established by the "49ers".

There are also historical maps available for each state dating from the early 1850s that help to identify what later became the Butterfield Route. Another excellent resource for Texas and New Mexico is the *Map of Texas and Parts of New Mexico* published in 1857 by the United States War Department Topographical Engineers. Additionally, several maps from the *Official Records Atlas of the Union and Confederate Armies* (1873) help to identify various Butterfield route segments and locations that were near or relevant to Civil War troop movements and encampments.

Ormsby contains some route descriptions and approximated mileages. Lang has transcribed several other contemporaneous reports that describe and give approximated mileages for a scattering of station locations.

Given that Postal Inspector Goddard Bailey's report to Postmaster General Brown was the "official word" on the itinerary and mileages in 1858; this author felt it most prudent and reliable to compare Ormsby, the Lang transcriptions and modern data to Bailey's mileage reports in setting a foundation for actual routes. It should be noted that the coaches ridden by Bailey were outfitted with an early version of an odometer (attached to a rear wheel of the coach) so as to render a "true" reading of the mileages for his official report to the Postmaster. For this reason, Bailey's measurements have been considered to be the most reliable "scientific data" as of 1858.

Where Ormsby and other journalistic chroniclers stated mileages that differed from (or were not measured by) Bailey, said data has been included in the reports -- but the journalists generally relied on the word of the drivers that the distance from "Station A" to "Station B" was a given number of miles.

Comparison of all of the early maps and reports helps to establish the Butterfield Route when these established earlier routes are aligned to Bailey's mileages and Ormsby's narratives. Further, comparing all of the early data to modern terrain maps and the array of modern Township / Range or GPS / geocache data and writings establishes reliable approximations of the original Butterfield Route.

Current satellite map overlays, terrain maps and topographic maps were then compared to Bailey's mileages, the known station locations and the modern field research to discover "the best roads and valleys" through a given area as the early data was overlaid onto modern maps.

Given these parameters and resources, the overall Butterfield Overland Mail Route data was plotted "station by station" onto a series of approximately 200 mapped segments. Each identifiable station location, notable topographic location, geological landmark and many relevant state historical markers were plotted on the individual maps -- thus creating a series of identifiable "dots" to be connected.

Using that series of "dots", what was known of the route was plotted point-to-point given the specific terrain of a given area using Bailey's measured mileages as a guideline for what "should be" the distance of the route segment.

Where specific route descriptions have been offered according to contemporaneous reports, those descriptions have been included in the segment reports.

In other cases, local field research (1930s to present) has detailed the original route through much of the overall trail. Where that data has been discovered, it has been included in the individual segment reports. On the other hand, there are a few cases where there still appear to be more than one candidate for the optimum "original route". Those specific cases have been discussed in the individual segment reports.

In some instances where the originating station locations remain obscure, there may be a slight margin of error in the segment mapping. Those cases have been specifically detailed in the individual segment narrative reports.

Reliable modern data (1930s to present has) also been collected and published that helps to identify many of the segment routings.

State by state, the most reliable modern data and descriptions regarding the original Butterfield Route discovered to-date have been recorded by:

• Missouri and Arkansas: Donald Mincke - *Chasing the Butterfield Overland Mail Stage* (2005 - self-published)

• Oklahoma: *Butterfield Centennial Committee Report - Butterfield Overland Mail* (1958 - Chronicles of Oklahoma; Oklahoma Historical Society

• Texas: A. C. Greene - 900 Miles On the Butterfield Trail (1994 - University of North Texas Press)

• New Mexico: George Hackler - *The Butterfield Trail in New Mexico* (2005 - Yucca Enterprises). Mr. Hackler also supplied a substantial amount of assistance and direction in establishing the segment routes and station sites in correspondence as of year 2010.

• Arizona: Gerald Ahnert - *Retracing the Butterfield Overland Trail through Arizona; a Guide to the Route of 1857-1861* (1973 - Westernlore Press). Once again, Mr. Ahnert also supplied a substantial amount of assistance and direction in establishing the segment routes and station sites in correspondence as of year 2010. • Data update as of March, 2013 – Mr. Ahnert has also published an updated and revised study, *The Butterfield Trail and Overland Mail Company in Arizona; 1858-1861* (2011 – Canastosa Publishing Co, Canastosa NY).

• Don Talbot - *Historical Guide to the Mormon Battalion and Butterfield Trail* (1992 - Western Lore Press)

California:

• Chris Wray of the Oregon - California Trails Association (OCTA) supplied a substantial amount of unpublished data and assistance based upon recent mapping and GIS data gathered by OCTA mapping teams in Southern California (Pilot Knob / Andrade CA to Warner Ranch). Said data was also compared to existing information published regarding the National Park Service de Anza Trail.

Through the Central Valley and into Northern California, the data appears to be more scattered. In that area, however, information establishing the early Camino Real and Mission Trail was used to verify the routes.

Where possible, local / regional experts were contacted and interviewed regarding the route through their area. While the individual contributions of area residents, town / county museums and local genealogical societies are too numerous to mention; three individuals deserve particular mention for their assistance.

In the preparation of these reports, draft copies of relevant reports and maps were reviewed by:

• Gerald Ahnert - author *Retracing the Butterfield Overland Trail through Arizona; a Guide to the Route of 1857-186*, and *The Butterfield Trail and Overland Mail Company in Arizona; 1858-1861;*

• George Hackler - author of *The Butterfield Trail in New Mexico;*

• Chris Wray - the Oregon California Trails Association (southern California and Mexico, Pilot Knob CA to Warner Ranch CA).

Where these individuals were contacted and comments received, their comments and suggestions were carefully considered and included in the resulting segment reports.

Efforts were also made to enlist the direct assistance of

• Donald Mincke - author of *Chasing the Butterfield Overland Mail Stage* (deceased as of November 11, 2007),

• A. C. Greene - author *900 Miles On the Butterfield Trail* (deceased as of April 5, 2002),

• Don Talbot - *Historical Guide to the Mormon Battalion and Butterfield Trail* (unable to locate 2008 to-date).

Narrative Reports

Of the approximately 200 individual narrative reports - these have been written to establish the criteria used in the identification of each route segment and the placement of the sites themselves.

Each of these reports contains a limited amount of interpretive data regarding the various stations and landmarks. Where local museums, state and federal historic parks and other notable modern facilities became apparent along the route, such locations were noted on the maps and segment reports.

While additional interpretive data has been collected for many of the stations and route segments has been discovered (including an initial image library of historical photographs and sketches of station sites and landmarks as well as recent photographs of restored sites and relevant historical markers), that full data is not included in these report. The focus of these reports is on the Butterfield Route rather than full interpretive descriptions of every station, stationmaster and notable bump in the road.

Said additional interpretive data can be readily included in future Preservation Planning and Implementation efforts.

It should be noted that in a few instances, definitive station locations could not be determined and had to be approximated based upon Bailey's mileage reports, contemporaneous historical mention, local field data and other available information. In some other instances, the actual station locations have been inundated by the later construction of reservoirs, obliterated by flooding or demolished to make way for urban and agricultural development. In yet a few other instances, there is conflicting data -- different resources have cited different locations for a single station. These anomalies have been noted in the individual maps and segment reports.

All of this data has been supplied to National Park Service Intermountain Region office in Santa Fe NM.

Into the Future

As an organizational criterion, this study was prepared on the assumption that it is "Phase One" of what is essentially a three-phase process in establishing the Butterfield Overland Mail Ox Bow Route National Historic Trail or other NPS Master Preservation Plan.

Said three phases were assumed to be:

• Phase One - Preliminary Route Establishment (based upon bibliographic resources and maps data)

• Phase Two - Preservation Planning (public meetings to establish a nationwide cooperative research and reporting effort, additional field research; onsite GPS readings for station locations; expansion of cooperative research with state and local experts on the Butterfield; inventory and (where needed) inspection of local archives to develop a Butterfield Image Library & definitive inventory of interpretive resources and other activities that would definitively confirm or correct the preliminary data for station locations and trail routing and facilitate the development of interpretive materials)

• Phase Three - Preservation Implementation (review of cooperative research results, development of signage and other interpretive materials regarding the relevant station locations and the route itself; consultation with state, regional and local tourism boards, Chambers of Commerce, economic development boards and other stakeholders to promote benefits and use of the Trail.)

The foundational theory of this "Phase One" process was quite simple. In order to facilitate "Phase Two" field research, one has to initially determine where "the field" is.

While most of the Butterfield Overland Mail stations and other notable landmarks can be placed with relative certainty, it is expected that modern in-depth historical and archaeological research along each of the route segments ("Phase Two") will help to definitively "pin" most of the relevant sites as well as the route itself. It is expected that this additional research may result in updated latitude and longitude placement of some stations in the future as well as some shifts in the approximated route.

It is also expected that during Phase Two (Preservation Planning) and Phase Three (Preservation Implementation) will be -- as this Texas boy would say -- "cussed and discussed" to the point at which Federal, State and Local cooperation establishes a thoroughly accurate reflection of this important transit and communication corridor.

Conclusion

The purpose of this preliminary Special Resource Study was to establish a series of definitively identified latitude / longitude "starting points" that are joined by the most accurate route mapping possible given best-available bibliographic and mapping data to-date.

That preliminary goal has been achieved.

In some cases, we are on the brink of losing parts of this important connection to our Unity as a Nation forever. Only additional cooperative research that is organized in conjunction with local jurisdictions and accessible via a National Inventory and database of Butterfield related Sites and the establishment of a readily accessible central archive will help us avoid losing these pieces of our shared National Identity to historical obscurity.

From this point, I would urge the House of Representatives, the Senate, The President of the United States and the Secretary of the Interior to authorize, fund and appropriate the continued detailed local research and the implementation of a Butterfield Overland Mail Oxbow Route (1858-1861) National Historic Trail followed by the implementation of an appropriate Master Preservation Plan.

- Kirby Sanders -
February 14, 2011

• Update as of April 2013 • The reports submitted to the National Park Service contain the maps herein. They did not include site photographs. Said photographs have been added during the preparation of this book.

Swiveller's Ranch (Arizona) to Fort Yuma (California)
December 23, 2010

April 23, 2011

Map Locator Number: 113 CA AZ

113. Snively's (a.k.a. "Swiveller's") Ranch / Gila City – near Dome AZ • Yuma County (N32° 45' 18.47", W114° 21' 39.71")

TO Fort Yuma - Winterhaven CA • Imperial County (N32° 43' 54.17", W114° 36' 55.83")

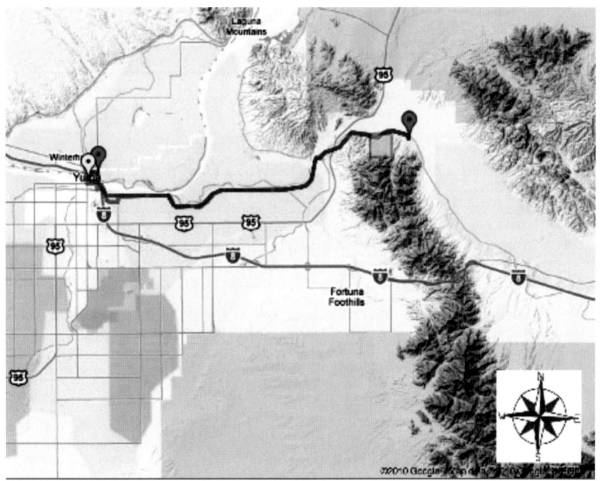

Approximate Actual Route, Snively's Ranch to Fort Yuma 18.5 miles
(1858 Bailey itinerary = 20 miles)

Secondary Landmarks:

Gila City / Monitor Gulch mining camp area - Township 8S, Range 21W, Section 11 - northwest corner - coordinates N32° 45' 27.51", W114° 23' 33.28"

Yuma Crossing - Yuma Crossing State Historical Park / Yuma Quartermaster Depot State Historic Park - coordinates N32 43' 32.27", W114 37' 19.42"

Notes:

From Snively's / Swiveller's Ranch / Gila City onward to Fort Yuma, the Butterfield Route tracks a southwesterly to westerly course near the Gila River along the historical corridor followed by Spanish explorer Juan Bautista de Anza (1775-1776); the Mormon Battalion (1846-1847); the road established by Col. James B. Leach (1857); and the course of the San Antonio - San Diego Stage route established by Skillman, Wasson, Birch et al. (1857).

In modern context, Ahnert (1973) includes a detailed map of the Snively's Station (Gila City) area toward the south and west. That map, however, does not include the entire route to Yuma Crossing and Fort Yuma.

Talbot (1992) includes a detailed map of the immediate Snively's Station vicinity that clearly concurs with Ahnert and the route as outlined in this segment map. He also includes a detailed map of the Yuma Crossing area. Talbot clearly overlays those segments on his maps of the Mormon Battalion Route through the area. He also indicates this route as having been explored by John Russell Bartlett during his U.S. - Mexico Boundary Survey as of June, 1852.

Comparing one map to another, those maps clearly indicate a southerly drop immediately to the west of Snively's / Swiveller's / Gila City into a westerly course onward to Yuma Crossing, although there is a significant gap between the joining points of those detailed maps.

The Oregon - California Trails Association (OCTA) has also done some field research and mapping of this segment. That data, supplied by Chris Wray of OCTA as of October 28, 2010, has also been taken into account. The detailed Wray / OCTA mapping data clearly indicates the same route as detailed by Ahnert, but it is sparse regarding the further westward segment to Yuma Crossing (which they identify correctly as "Jaeger Ferry").

Portions of this segment can be found on some modern maps identified as "Route of the Butterfield Stage" to the point at which it enters the broad plain approaching what is now Yuma. That terminus is in the vicinity of what is now S Madonna Road at State Highway 95 and appears to be the same terminus used by the Wray / OCTA and Ahnert maps.

Thereafter, the Butterfield Route appears to skirt various tributaries of the Colorado River on an essentially westerly track along a meandering course toward a brief northwesterly approach to Yuma Crossing.

The Butterfield entered California by way of Yuma Crossing / Jaeger's Ferry at the Colorado River from Arizona to Fort Yuma in California.

Talbot reports the Butterfield coaches "crossed the Colorado River on a ferry operated by Louis J.F. Yager (or Jaeger) at a cost of five dollars for a four-horse team."

Ormsby specifically mentions Mr. "Yager" and his ferry, noting that "The boat is a sort of flatboat, and is propelled by the rapid current, being kept on its course by pulleys running on a rope stretched across the river."

Yuma Crossing / Yager's Ferry / Jaeger's Ferry was located in the vicinity of what is now Yuma Crossing State Historical Park / Yuma Quartermaster Depot State Historic Park (Arizona - approximate coordinates N32° 43' 32.27", W114° 37' 19.42").

The Wray / OCTA mapping data places "Jaeger Ferry" at coordinates N32° 43' 42.16", W114° 37' 02.42" -- slightly east of the Quartermaster Depot State Park on the modern Kumeyaay Highway / Interstate 8.

The Yuma Crossing State Historical Park / Yuma Quartermaster Depot State Historic Park main office and visitor center is located at 201 N. 4th Avenue, Yuma, and is the site of several buildings and displays from the old Army Quartermasters' post established here. According to information from the Arizona State Parks:

> ... supplies were unloaded near the stone reservoir just west of the commanding officer's quarters and hauled up on a track running from the river dock through the center of the storehouse. They were shipped north on river steamers and overland by mule drawn freight wagons. The depot quartered up to 900 mules and a crew of teamsters to handle them. The Southern Pacific Railroad reached Yuma in 1877 and heralded the end of the Quartermaster Depot and Fort Yuma. The railroad reached Tucson in 1880, and the functions were moved to Fort Lowell in Tucson.

> The Signal Corps established a telegraph and weather station here in 1875. The supply depot was terminated by the Army in 1883, and the

pumps, steam engines and equipment were sent to Fort Lowell near Tucson, but the Signal Corps remained until 1891. The U.S. Weather Service was established as a separate agency and operated at the depot site until 1949.

The Yuma Crossing Quartermaster's Depot is listed on the National Register of Historic Places (Yuma Crossing and Associated Sites; 1966 - #66000197).

According to the National Register documentation, "First used by Native Americans, this natural crossing served as a significant transportation gateway on the Colorado River during the Spanish Colonial and U.S. westward expansion periods. The surviving buildings of the Yuma Quartermaster Depot and Arizona Territorial Prison are the key features on the Arizona side of the border; across the river, in California, stand the surviving buildings of Fort Yuma, an Army outpost that guarded the crossing from 1850 to 1885."

The next station location is at the original site of "Camp Yuma," later improved to become Fort Yuma near coordinates (N32° 43' 54.17", W114° 36' 55.83").

Ormsby specifically mentions Fort Yuma. Bailey lists Fort Yuma as a mileage point.

Information from the California State Military Department, California State Military Museum, reports that Fort Yuma was

> First established on November 27, 1850, it was originally located in the bottoms near the Colorado River, less than a mile below the mouth of the Gila. In March 1851 the post was moved to a small elevation on the Colorado's west bank, opposite the present city of Yuma, Arizona, on the site of the former Mission Puerto de la Purísima Concepción. This site had been occupied by Camp Calhoun, named for John C. Calhoun, established on October 2, 1849, by 1st lieutenant Cave J. Couts, 1st Dragoons, for the boundary survey party led by 2nd Lieutenant Amiel W. Whipple, Corps of Topographical Engineers. A ferry service, maintained by the soldiers for the survey party's convenience, also accommodated emigrants. Fort Yuma was established to protect the southern emigrant travel route to California and to attempt control of the warlike Yuma Indians in the surrounding 100 mile area.

Established by Captain Samuel P. Heintzelman, 2nd Infantry, it was originally named Camp Independence. In March 1851, when the post was moved to its permanent site, its name was changed to Camp Yuma. A year later the post was designated Fort Yuma. In June 1851 the Army virtually abandoned the post because of the high costs incurred in maintaining it, and it was completely abandoned on December 6, 1851, when its commissary was practically empty of provisions.

The post, however, was reoccupied by Captain Heintzelman on February 29, 1852. In 1864 the Quartermaster Corps erected a depot on the left bank of the Colorado, below the mouth of the Gila River. When the extension of the railroad system obviated the need of a supply depot, Fort Yuma was abandoned on May 16, 1883. The reservation was transferred to the Interior Department on July 22, 1884. Today, the site of the military reservation is occupied by the Fort Yuma Indian School and a mission.

There are two historical markers of note located at the Butterfield period site of Fort Yuma near present-day 350 Picacho Road in Winterhaven, California.

The first is a California State Historical Marker (#806). It tells us "Fort Yuma - Originally called Camp Calhoun, the site was first used as a U.S. military post in 1849. A fire destroyed the original buildings. By 1855 the barracks had been rebuilt. Called Camp Yuma in 1852, it became Fort Yuma after reconstruction. Transferred to the Department of the Interior and the Quechan Indian Tribe in 1884, it became a boarding school operated by the Catholic Church until 1900."

The second relevant State Historical Resources Commission Marker (#350) recognizes the original Mission site. It reads "Mission La Purísima Concepción (Site of) - In October 1780, Father Francisco Garcés and companions began Mission La Purísima Concepción. The mission/pueblo site was inadequately supported. Colonists ignored Indian rights, usurped the best lands, and destroyed Indian crops. Completely frustrated and disappointed, the Quechans (Yumas) and their allies destroyed Concepción on July 17-19, 1781."

This marker is near the Saint Thomas Indian Mission, still a church and Catholic Services location serving the local Native American population. Information from the Diocese of San Diego, which administers the Mission, notes "The first mission at Ft. Yuma was named Purísima Concepción, established in 1780. It became a U.S. military outpost in the 19th century

24

and was revived as an active mission again in 1919. The current church, St. Thomas Indian Mission, was dedicated in 1923."

The Ahnert, Talbot and Wray / OCTA data terminates at Yuma Crossing Arizona and does not include specifics regarding Fort Yuma in California.

References:

Arizona State Parks; *Yuma Quartermaster Depot State Historic Park*; Internet publication accessible at http://azstateparks.com/parks/YUQU/index.html (accessed August 8, 2010)

Bailey, Goddard; *California -- Arrival of the Overland Mail -- Itinerary of the Route*; as reported by newspaper article; *New York Times* (NY) - October 14, 1858.

Bailey, Goddard; *Report to Postmaster General A.V. Brown - Full itinerary as reported by De Bow's Review and Industrial Resources, Statistics etc.*; published by *De Bow's Review*; New Orleans and Washington City; 1858. See specifically *Internal Improvements - 1. Wagon Road to the Pacific*; pp. 719-721. Internet accessible at http://books.google.com/books?id=5CYoAAAAYAAJ&pg=PA720&lpg=PA720&dq=Cienega+de+los+Pimas&source=bl&ots=_5lZw_Bq23&sig=T6scCb8cpbY7KwjxpYoNvZpcgvI&hl=en&ei=i6KnS6KNOIr2M5yprIED&sa=X&oi=book_result&ct=result&resnum=2&ved=0CAwQ6AEwAQ#v=onepage&q=Cienega%20de%20los%20Pimas&f=false (accessed March 22, 2010).

California State Military Department; *Fort Yuma (Including Camp Calhoun, Camp Independence, Camp Yuma, Yuma Quartermaster Depot)*; Internet publication accessible at http://www.militarymuseum.org/FtYuma.html (accessed August 8, 2010).

California State Parks - Office of Historic Preservation; *California Historical Landmarks*; Internet database - http://www.parks.ca.gov/default.asp?page_id=21387 (accessed April 4, 2010).

Conkling, Roscoe P. and Margaret B.; *The Butterfield Overland Mail, 1857–1869* (3 vols.); Glendale, CA: A. H. Clark Company, 1947.

National Park Service; *Juan Bautista de Anza National Historic Trail Guide, Yuma County AZ*; Internet publication available at http://www.solideas.com/DeAnza/TrailGuide/ (accessed July 28, 2010).

National Park Service; *Juan Bautista de Anza National Historic Trail Guide, Imperial County CA*; Internet publication available at http://www.solideas.com/DeAnza/TrailGuide/ (accessed July 28, 2010).

National Register of Historic Places; *National Register Locations by State*; Internet publication; accessible at

http://www.nationalregisterofhistoricplaces.com/state.html (accessed May 3, 2010).

Oregon - California Trails Association; *Learn. Connect. Preserve.*; Internet publication accessible at http://www.octa-trails.org/ (accessed October 9, 2010).

Ormsby, Waterman L.; *The Butterfield Overland Mail (Only Through Passenger on the First Westbound Stage)*; original publications *New York Herald* (NY) Sep 26 - Nov 19, 1858; republished by Henry E. Huntington Library and Art Gallery, San Marino CA, 1942 – 1998.

Talbot, Dan; *Historical Guide to the Mormon Battalion and Butterfield Trail;* Westernlore Press, 1992.

**Historical lithograph of Fort Yuma 1875.
Litho by George Baker.**

Fort Yuma to Pilot Knob Mesa
April 24, 2011

114. Fort Yuma - near Winterhaven, CA • Imperial County (N32° 43' 54.17", W114° 36' 55.83")

TO Pilot Knob Mesa - near Andrade CA • Imperial County (N32° 43' 17.55, W114° 43' 31.47")

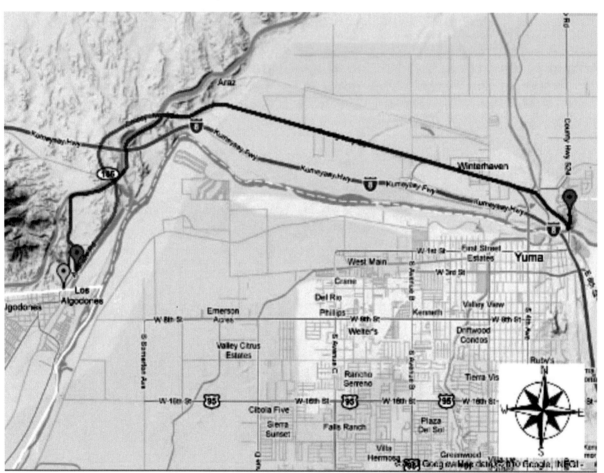

Approximate Actual Route Fort Yuma to Pilot Knob 8.5 miles.

(1858 Bailey itinerary says 10 miles)

Secondary Landmarks:

Pilot Knob Station per Chris Wray (Oregon - California Trails Association) - coordinates N32° 43' 06.06", W114° 43' 42.03"

Notes:

The Butterfield route through this segment continues to track the earlier de Anza (1775-1776) and Mormon Battalion (1846-1847) routes. It also tracks the 1852 route used by John Russell Bartlett in his U.S. - Mexico Boundary Survey and the 1857 course of the San Antonio - San Diego Stage route established by Skillman, Wasson, Birch et al.

The detailed Wray / OCTA mapping data does not indicate a detailed route breakdown or a location marker for Fort Yuma.

In general terms, the Butterfield Route followed a westerly course along what is the northern bank of the Colorado River in this area. The route then "turned the bend" in the river and followed a direct southwesterly course along the western bank of the Colorado River.

The first Butterfield station location beyond Fort Yuma was Pilot Knob Station near the Pilot Knob Mesa in the vicinity of present-day Andrade. Some California researchers maintain that Pilot Knob Mesa may have been the first landmark in California to have been noted by the Spanish, possibly having been visited by Hernando de Alarcón Melchor Díaz in 1540 as part of Coronado's explorations seeking the Seven Cities of Cibola.

While there is some disagreement among researchers and scholars, it is quite possible that the Pilot Knob Station was located at the early site of the Misión y Pueblo San Pedro y San Pablo de Bicuñer. There seems to be documentary evidence that this Mission was located near the Pilot Knob Mesa; however, some researchers place the mission site further north.

Franciscan monks from Mexico built two missions, Misión y Pueblo San Pedro y San Pablo de Bicuñer and Misión Puerto La Purisima Concepción de la Virgén Santisima, near Pilot Knob during the 1700s to serve as way stations on the trail from Mexico to the California missions farther west and north.

In 1781 a group of colonists with 1,000 head of cattle arrived in the area on their way to establish a new settlement at what would later become the city of Los Angeles. The native Quechan Indians, however, believed the settlers sought to settle at Pilot Knob and take their land. The Indians attacked San Pedro y San Pablo de Bicuñer and another small mission to the north in July of that year. During that incident Captain Don Fernando Rivera, Father Francis Tomás Hermenogildo Garcés, and most of the men and boys in the emigrant party were killed. More than 100 settlers were killed in all and about 75 were held captive. The captives were eventually ransomed by a party led by Pedro Fages in 1782.

Misión y Pueblo San Pedro y San Pablo de Bicuñer and the nearby Misión Puerto La Purisima Concepción de la Virgén Santisima were not substantial. The buildings at the sites were made of wood and no ruins of either site remain.

Whether at a former mission site or not, Ormsby is very clear that the coaches passed toward the east and then south of Pilot Knob Mesa. He described the mesa as "… a mountain which extends nearly to the very verge of the river, leaving but a narrow pass for the road."

Bailey specifically identifies Pilot Knob as a station in his itinerary and mileages.

Mildred Brooke Hoover, Hero Eugene Rensch and Ethel Grace Rensch specifically discuss Pilot Knob as a Butterfield location in their book *Historic Spots in California* as does Elizabeth Harris in *The Valley Imperial*.

Hoover specifically notes that the Butterfield Route substantially followed the route of the de Anza explorations of 1775-1776 through this area.

George Wharton James, in *The Wonders of the Colorado Desert,* also discusses the importance of Pilot Knob in the overall history of the area.

Talbot also mentions Pilot Knob as a Butterfield Station in his appendices, although he does not indicate locations or include detailed maps for segments outside of Arizona.

The Wray / OCTA mapping data reports an approximate location of the Pilot Knob Station immediately at the U.S. Customs Service facility on the border with Mexico on Andrade Road (coordinates N32° 43' 6.00", W114° 43' 42.00"). That location is approximately 1500 feet southwest of the report coordinates (N32 43' 17.55, W114 43 31.47").

References:

Bailey, Goddard; *California -- Arrival of the Overland Mail -- Itinerary of the Route*; as reported by newspaper article; New York Times (NY) - October 14, 1858

Bailey, Goddard; *Report to Postmaster General A.V. Brown - Full itinerary as reported by De Bow's Review and Industrial Resources, Statistics etc;* published by De Bow's Review; New Orleans and Washington City; 1858. See specifically *Internal Improvements - 1. Wagon Road to the Pacific;* pp 719-721. Internet accessible at
http://books.google.com/books?id=5CYoAAAAYAAJ&pg=PA720&lpg=PA720&dq=Cienega+de+los+Pimas&source=bl&ots=_5lZw_Bq23&sig=T6scCb8cpbY7KwjxpYoNvZpcgvI&hl=en&ei=i6KnS6KNOIr2M5yprIED&sa=X&oi=book_result&ct=result&resnum=2&ved=0CAwQ6AEwAQ#v=onepage&q=Cienega%20de%20los%20Pimas&f=false (accessed March 22, 2010)

Bartlett, John Russell; *Personal Narrative of Explorations and Incidents in Texas, New Mexico, California, Sonora and Chihuahua - Vol. One;* D. Appleton and Company; *New York; 1854*

Conkling, Roscoe P. and Margaret B.; *The Butterfield Overland Mail, 1857–1869* (3 vols); Glendale, CA: A. H. Clark Company, 1947.

Harris, Elizabeth; *The Valley Imperial;* Imperial Valley Historical Society; Imperial CA; 1956 - 1958 (reprinted 1991)

Hoover, Mildred Brooke, Hero Eugene Rensch and Ethel Grace Rensch; *Historic Spots in California;* Stanford University Press; Stanford CA; 1932 (rev 1948)

James, George Wharton; *The Wonders of the Colorado Desert (Southern California);* Little, Brown & Company; Boston; 1906

Internet accessible at Google Books:
http://books.google.com/books?id=clgTAAAAYAAJ&printsec=frontcover&dq=Wonders+of+the+colorado&source=bl&ots=-MjgRLp6hk&sig=VIUUDP3kTVmTU53kaRo9FQi8HDw&hl=en&ei=nh6MS4X5IoSINOjSlW4&sa=X&oi=book_result&ct=result&resnum=7&ved=0CCQQ6AEwBg#v=onepage&q=&f=false

National Park Service; *Juan Bautista de Anza National Historic Trail Guide Imperial County CA);* Internet publication available at http://www.solideas.com/DeAnza/TrailGuide/Imperial/index.html (accessed July 28, 2010)

Oregon - California Trails Association; *Learn. Connect. Preserve.*; Internet publication accessible at http://www.octa-trails.org/ (accessed October 9, 2010)

Ormsby, Waterman L.; *The Butterfield Overland Mail (Only Through Passenger on the First Westbound Stage)*; original publications New York Herald (NY) Sep 26 - Nov 19, 1858; republished by Henry E. Huntington Library and Art Gallery, San Marino CA, 1942 - 1998

Talbot, Don; *Historical Guide to the Mormon Battalion and Butterfield Trail;* Westernlore Press, 1992

View of Pilot Knob Mesa from vicinity of Pilot Knob station site (N32.792, W114.619). Photo by Fred Yeck (2006).

Pilot Knob Mesa to Indian Wells
April 24, 2011

Pilot Knob Mesa - near Andrade CA • Imperial County (N32° 43' 17.55, W114° 43 31.47")

TO Indian Wells - near Seeley, CA • Imperial County (N32° 44' 37.20", W115° 38' 58.20")

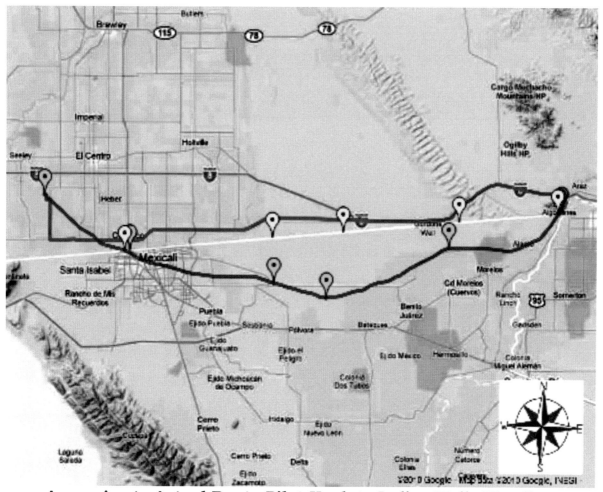

Approximate Actual Route Pilot Knob to Indian Wells 59 miles.

(see detailed breakdown in "Notes" below for comparison to 1858 Bailey)

32

Secondary Landmarks:

Border Monument 207 (Butterfield Route enters Mexico) - Andrade CA - approximate coordinates N32° 43' 4.86", W114° 43' 53.52"

Border Monument 210 (Cooke's Wells - U.S. side of border) - N32° 42' 21.50", W114° 54' 36.10"

Cooke's Wells in Mexico per Chris Wray; Oregon - California Trails Association (OCTA) - approximate coordinates N32° 40' 09.60", W114° 55' 39.00"

Border Monument 214 (Gardner's Wells - U.S. side of border) - N32° 41' 30.43", W115° 07' 01.38"

Gardner's Wells in Mexico per Chris Wray; Oregon - California Trails Association (OCTA) - approximate coordinates N32° 35' 51.00", W115° 08' 54.00"

Border Monument 216 (Alamo Mocho - U.S. side of border) - N32° 40' 58.38", W115° 14' 39.91"

Alamo Mocho in Mexico per Chris Wray; Oregon - California Trails Association (OCTA) - approximate coordinates N32° 37' 46.20, W115° 14' 27.22"

Alamo Mocho alternative possibility in Mexico - N32° 37' 306.60" W115° 14' 29.40"

Border Monument 221 (Butterfield Route reenters USA) - N32° 39' 51.12", W115° 30' 20.73"

Notes:

The ongoing Butterfield Route continues to track the earlier de Anza (1775-1776) and Mormon Battalion (1846-1847) routes. It also tracks the 1852 route used by John Russell Bartlett in his U.S. - Mexico Boundary Survey and the 1857 course of the San Antonio - San Diego Stage route established by Skillman, Wasson, Birch et al.

The original Butterfield Route segment from Pilot Knob westward drops into what is now (and was in 1858) Mexico through the next several stations. In general terms it follows a southwesterly to northwesterly arc from Andrade CA to the cities of Mexicali (Mexico) and Calexico CA onward to Indian Wells.

Three stations (Cooke's Wells, Gardner's Wells and Alamo Mocho) were in Mexico at the time they were used by the Butterfield and are located in Mexico today. For the purposes of this report, we have identified the approximate locations of the stations within Mexico. The actual route and the proper station sites in this report have been plotted on the Mexico side of the border. The auto route stays to the U.S. side of the border and identifies the nearest corresponding border monuments to each of those stations.

Ormsby and Bailey both outline this route through Mexico.

The Butterfield coaches crossed into Mexico near the United States / Mexico Border Monument #207. U.S. Coast and Geodetic Survey data places Monument #207 at coordinates N32° 43' 4.86", W114° 43' 53.52". This approximates the point at which Algodones Road passes out of the United States and becomes Calle 186 approaching Vicente Guerrero, Mexico.

According to *The Valley Imperial* by Elizabeth Harris, "From the Pilot Knob Station, the trail wound south crossing the International Boundary at a point now known as Algodones then headed southwest 14 miles, skirting the sand dunes and following the channel of the Alamo [river] to a point called Cooke's Wells where a stage station was established by Warren Hall. Wells previously dug by the [United States] army were cleaned and enlarged, providing ample water."

Harris places Cooke's Wells at "about six miles south of [United States / Mexico Border] Monument 210." U.S. Coast and Geodetic Survey data places that monument at coordinates N32° 42' 21.50", W114° 54' 36.10". In correspondence as of October 29, 2010, Chris Wray of OCTA, in correspondence of October 29,2010, notes that their field and mapping teams place this station site at coordinates N32° 40' 09.60", W114° 55' 39.00".

Bailey (1858) specifically notes the distance between Pilot Knob and "Cook's Wells" as 18 miles.

Harris then reports that the trail tracked "... for 14 miles to the next station stop. Gardner's Wells [was] located approximately 5.8 miles south of Monument 214, or, four and one-half miles southeast of a later well known watering place of Seven Wells."

The U.S. Coast and Geodetic Survey data places Border Monument 214 at coordinates N32° 41' 30.43", W115° 07' 01.38". Wray and the OCTA researchers place the actual Gardner's Wells station site at coordinates N32° 35' 51.00", W115° 08' 54.00".

Returning to Harris' documentation, "From Gardner's Wells station, the trail wound almost due west for 12 miles to Alamo Mocho, the next station, six miles south of Monument 216. The site of this station was on what appears to be the bank of the old Alamo River bed now known as Beltran Slough."

U.S. Coast and Geodetic Survey data places Monument 216 at coordinates N32° 40' 58.38", W115° 14' 39.91". Wray notes that the OCTA field and mapping teams place the Alamo Mocho station site at coordinates N32° 37' 36.60" W115° 14' 29.40".

Bailey (1858) does not mention Gardener's Wells but cites a through-mileage to "Alamo Wells" as 22 miles.

As the coaches came out of Mexico and back into the United States, Harris says "From Alamo Mocho the trail led west to the New River Crossing, turned north and followed the west bank of the dry wash to Monument 221, crossing the border into the United States near this point. U.S. Coast and Geodetic Survey data places Monument 221 at coordinates N32° 39' 51.12", W115° 30' 20.73"; which point lies just west of the present-day border crossing at Calexico, California.

Wray and the OCTA team measured the re-entry location indicated by Harris approximately 900 yards due east of the USC&GS coordinates for Border Monument 221.

Bartlett (1854 publication) also discusses having camped at a wellsite at "Alamo Mucho" and the occasional appearance and disappearance of the "New River" in this area. From Bartlett's descriptions, it appears that the New River and the Alamo River in the 1850s were arroyos that only became "rivers" during periods of substantial rainfall to the north.

Talbot mentions Cooke's Well, Alamo Mocho and Indian Wells as Butterfield Stations in his appendices, although he does not indicate locations or include detailed maps for segments outside of Arizona.

The Indian Wells Station, according to all available research, is now beneath the course of the New River near Seeley CA. The unincorporated community of Seeley is near the former town of Silsbee and located near the former site of Blue Lake. According to some sources, Seeley is the site of the original Silsbee settlement; however, other descriptions indicate that Silsbee was on the eastern shore of Blue Lake to the south of modern Seeley whilst the Indian Wells stage station was to the west of Blue Lake -- and given that Blue Lake no longer exists, it is difficult to get a true reading on this location.

Bailey (1858) specifically mentions the next station at Indian Wells, indicating "no water" -- but offers no notation of specific route or mileage from Alamo Mocho.

Hoover mentions Indian Wells as being in the vicinity of Silsbee / Seeley CA.

A copy of the quarterly journal *Out West* for January - June 1903 (Los Angeles, CA - ed. Chas. F. Lummis) contains mention of Silsbee and Blue Lake at that time on page 140. "The town of Silsbee is situated on the eastern shore of Blue Lake, one of the most charming bodies of fresh water on the Pacific Coast. Blue Lake is only about one mile in length and half a mile wide but it is well stocked with fish and surrounded by mesquite timber which will afford shade for a fine boulevard encircling the entire lake."

Apparently, the boulevard was never built. In 1905, a massive flood of the Colorado River inundated the Salton Sink to the north, creating the Salton Sea and generating massive flooding throughout Imperial County. As a result of those floods, which took place continuously for the next two years, the permanent New River and Alamo River were created from Salton Sea outflow, and Blue Lake (as a separate identifiable entity) disappeared into the overall watershed.

George Wharton James' *Wonders of the Colorado Desert* contains a description of the ruins of Indian Wells Station shortly before they were washed away in another flood during 1906: "Two miles from Silsbee, on the east side of the New River, hides a remnant of the old adobe stage station Indian Wells. This used to be a strong and massive building with walls like a fortress and completely surrounded by a protecting wall. Inside this wall was plenty of water and wood, so that the station-keeper was safe from Indian attacks. How forcefully the lesson is driven home here, in sight of the green fields of cultivated ranches, how the romance of the stagecoach days has given place to the romance of the plow. On every hand now are evidences of human industry and prosperity."

In his 2010 correspondence, Wray reported that the OCTA research and mapping teams have placed the Indian Wells within the New River arroyo approximately five miles due southeast of Seeley in the vicinity of Silsbee Road at coordinates N32° 44' 37.20", W115° 38' 58.20" -- which coordinates have been used for this report.

• Data update as of March 2013 • Based on the Conklings' data, researcher Fred Yeck places the Indian Wells Station site approximately 2.6

miles northwest of the Wray / OCTA site on Drew Road at coordinates N32° 45' 35", W115° 41' 23"

An additional resource consideration for the development of Planning and Implementation data on this segment is the Imperial County Pioneers Society in Holtville CA.

References:

Bailey, Goddard; *California -- Arrival of the Overland Mail -- Itinerary of the Route*; as reported by newspaper article; New York Times (NY) - October 14, 1858

Bailey, Goddard; *Report to Postmaster General A.V. Brown - Full itinerary as reported by De Bow's Review and Industrial Resources, Statistics etc;* published by De Bow's Review; New Orleans and Washington City; 1858. See specifically *Internal Improvements - 1. Wagon Road to the Pacific*; pp 719-721. Internet accessible at http://books.google.com/books?id=5CYoAAAAYAAJ&pg=PA720&lpg=PA720&dq=Cienega+de+los+Pimas&source=bl&ots=_5lZw_Bq23&sig=T6scCb8cpbY7K wjxpYoNvZpcgvI&hl=en&ei=i6KnS6KNOIr2M5yprIED&sa=X&oi=book_result& ct=result&resnum=2&ved=0CAwQ6AEwAQ#v=onepage&q=Cienega%20de%20 los%20Pimas&f=false (accessed March 22, 2010)

Bartlett, John Russell; *Personal Narrative of Explorations and Incidents in Texas, New Mexico, California, Sonora and Chihuahua - Vol. One*; D. Appleton and Company; *New York; 1854*

Conkling, Roscoe P. and Margaret B.; *The Butterfield Overland Mail, 1857– 1869* (3 vols); Glendale, CA: A. H.   Clark Company, 1947.

Harris, Elizabeth; *The Valley Imperial*; Imperial Valley Historical Society; Imperial CA; 1956 - 1958 (reprinted 1991)

Hoover, Mildred Brooke, Hero Eugene Rensch and Ethel Grace Rensch; *Historic Spots in California*; Stanford University Press; Stanford CA; 1932 (rev 1948)

James, George Wharton; *The Wonders of the Colorado Desert (Southern California)*; Little, Brown & Company; Boston; 1906

Internet accessible at Google Books: http://books.google.com/books?id=clgTAAAAYAAJ&printsec=frontcover&dq= Wonders+of+the+colorado&source=bl&ots=- MjgRLp6hk&sig=VIUUDP3kTVmTU53kaRo9FQi8HDw&hl=en&ei=nh6MS4X5I

oSINOjSlW4&sa=X&oi=book_result&ct=result&resnum=7&ved=0CCQQ6AEw
Bg#v=onepage&q=&f=false

Lummis, Charles Fletcher, *Out West Quarterly*, January-June 1903, Los Angeles CA

National Park Service; *Juan Bautista de Anza National Historic Trail Guide Imperial County CA)*; Internet publication available at http://www.solideas.com/DeAnza/TrailGuide/Imperial/index.html (accessed July 28, 2010)

Oregon - California Trails Association; *Learn. Connect. Preserve.*; Internet publication accessible at http://www.octa-trails.org/ (accessed October 9, 2010)

Ormsby, Waterman L.; *The Butterfield Overland Mail (Only Through Passenger on the First Westbound Stage)*; original publications New York Herald (NY) Sep 26 - Nov 19, 1858; republished by Henry E. Huntington Library and Art Gallery, San Marino CA, 1942 - 1998

Talbot, Don; *Historical Guide to the Mormon Battalion and Butterfield Trail;* Westernlore Press, 1992

Indian wells near Silsbee

**Indian Wells stage station (Silsbee CA).
Sketch by Carl Eytel (1907). From Gorge Wharton
James - The Wonders of the Colorado Desert
Vol. II.**

Indian Wells to Carrizo Creek Station
April 24, 2011

Indian Wells - near Seeley, CA • Imperial County (N32° 44' 37.20", W115° 38' 58.20")

TO Carrizo Creek Station - Anza Borrego Desert State Park • San Diego County (N32° 52' 25.16", W116° 8' 17.23")

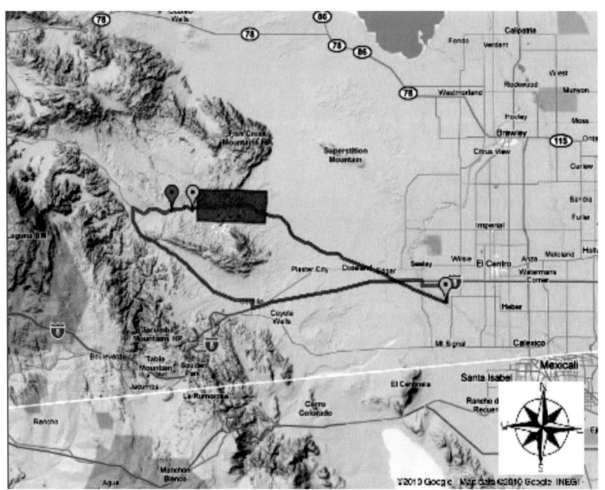

Approximate Actual Route Indian Wells to Carrizo Creek 32 miles.

(1858 Bailey itinerary says 32 miles)

Secondary Landmarks:

Carrizo Impact Area (closed to the public) - east of Anza Borrego Desert State Park - between approximate coordinates N32 52' 07.53", W115° 58' 06.70" to approximate coordinates N32° 52' 49.23", W116 05' 06.57".

Notes:

The Butterfield route through this segment tracks the de Anza (1775-1776) route to a point north of Plaster City and southwest of Superstition Mountain. At that point, the Butterfield route turns west via the Carrizo Wash into what is now Anza Borrego Desert State Park while the de Anza angled northward.

The westward divergence of the Butterfield route from the de Anza directly tracks the 1846-1847 Mormon Battalion route toward San Diego as well as the 1852 route used by John Russell Bartlett in his U.S. - Mexico Boundary Survey and the 1857 course of the San Antonio - San Diego Stage route established by Skillman, Wasson, Birch et al.

The segment from just north of Plaster City CA into the Anza Borrego Desert State Park can be found marked as the "Old Overland Stage Route" on some modern maps.

The original route to the Carrizo Springs Butterfield Station through this area is, in part, inaccessible to the public. The station site is accessible within California's Anza Borrego Desert State Park. However, approximately seven miles of the original route immediately to the east of the station pass through what is referred to as the "Carrizo Impact Area." This area was used as the "receiving end" of a live-ammunition training and testing ground for air-to-ground bombing runs by the United States military from World War II through the Korean War. In less cryptic terms, "Impact Area" means "old military bombing range with unexploded live artillery shells scattered all over the place that spontaneously and unpredictably 'cook off' and blow up every now and again."

In the case of the Butterfield Route through this area, the old saw about being "close enough for horseshoes and hand grenades" applies literally. The "Carrizo Impact Area" and the Butterfield Route that passes through it are closed to the public -- for safety reasons.

During a telephone interview with Louise Jee (GIS Department of the Anza Borrego Desert State Park) on November 16, 2010, she confirmed that the original Butterfield Route is closed to the public from approximate coordinates N32° 52' 07.53", W115° 58' 06.70" westward to approximate coordinates N32° 52' 49.23", W116° 05' 06.57".

Jee also stated that the area within the Carrizo Impact Area contains environmentally sensitive areas that would be destroyed as the result of over-trafficking and / or the detonation of the old military materiel. A situation she referred to as a "double-edged sword."

It should also be noted that the Anza Borrego Desert State Park has taken steps to establish the Butterfield Route through the entire park as a recognized Cultural Preserve and should be closely consulted for cooperation during establishment of any National Trail or other Master Preservation Plan.

The Carrizo Creek Station coordinates for this report (N32° 52' 25.16", W116° 8' 17.23") represent the nearest point to the actual station site one can reach via improved roads in the area that is open to public access. As noted below, the station site is accessible to the public but only by way of a poor, unimproved road.

Wray and the OCTA field research and mapping teams locate the actual site approximately 2.2 miles east of the report location at coordinates N32° 52' 30.39, W116° 06' 02.57". Jee confirmed the Wray / OCTA coordinate location for this site. Jee also confirmed the overall validity of the Wray / OCTA routes and site readings throughout this area.

Hoover notes that the Butterfield route through Carrizo Creek and the remainder of the Anza Borrego Desert State Park to Warner Springs was originally explored by Pedro Fages in 1772.

Further, Hoover reports, "Santiago Arguello, in pursuit of Indian horse thieves, rediscovered this trail in 1825. In January, 1826, the Mexican government sent Romualdo Pacheco, Lieutenant of Engineers, to investigate it and with his approval it was approved as an official mail route. ... Probably the first Americans to come this way were David E. Jackson and his party of fur traders, who had come overland from Santa Fe in 1831. Later it came to be known as the Emigrant Trail and formed a part of the Southern Overland Trail, a much-traveled route from the East into California in the '40s and '50s."

Bailey and Ormsby both specifically mention the Carrizo Creek Station. James writes specifically of the Carrizo Creek Station and includes a hand-drawn sketch of the station ruins circa 1906.

Talbot also mentions the Carrizo Creek Station in his appendices.

By the 1932 writing of Hoover's *Historic Spots*, "... little more than a heap of mud remains today."

The actual stage station route is semi-accessible. The road to the site is not improved. It is severely rutted and rocky and prone to occasional flooding. Most reports indicate the last half-mile of park road approaching the station site is only navigable by foot or four-wheel drive vehicles (at best). For those without access to such vehicles, the road is reported to be passable up to the "Y" intersection where Sweeney Road meets the Great Southern Overland Trail Route road.

References:

Bailey, Goddard; *California -- Arrival of the Overland Mail -- Itinerary of the Route*; as reported by newspaper article; New York Times (NY) - October 14, 1858

Bailey, Goddard; *Report to Postmaster General A.V. Brown - Full itinerary as reported by De Bow's Review and Industrial Resources, Statistics etc;* published by De Bow's Review; New Orleans and Washington City; 1858. See specifically *Internal Improvements - 1. Wagon Road to the Pacific;* pp 719-721. Internet accessible at http://books.google.com/books?id=5CYoAAAAYAAJ&pg=PA720&lpg=PA720& dq=Cienega+de+los+Pimas&source=bl&ots=_5lZw_Bq23&sig=T6scCb8cpbY7K wjxpYoNvZpcgvI&hl=en&ei=i6KnS6KNOIr2M5yprIED&sa=X&oi=book_result& ct=result&resnum=2&ved=0CAwQ6AEwAQ#v=onepage&q=Cienega%20de%20 los%20Pimas&f=false (accessed March 22, 2010)

Bartlett, John Russell; *Personal Narrative of Explorations and Incidents in Texas, New Mexico, California, Sonora and Chihuahua - Vol. One*; D. Appleton and Company; *New York; 1854*

Conkling, Roscoe P. and Margaret B.; *The Butterfield Overland Mail, 1857– 1869* (3 vols); Glendale, CA: A. H.   Clark Company, 1947.

Harris, Elizabeth; *The Valley Imperial*; Imperial Valley Historical Society; Imperial CA; 1956 - 1958 (reprinted 1991)

Hoover, Mildred Brooke, Hero Eugene Rensch and Ethel Grace Rensch; *Historic Spots in California*; Stanford University Press; Stanford CA; 1932 (rev 1948)

James, George Wharton; *The Wonders of the Colorado Desert (Southern California)*; Little, Brown & Company; Boston; 1906

Internet accessible at google books:
http://books.google.com/books?id=clgTAAAAYAAJ&printsec=frontcover&dq=
Wonders+of+the+colorado&source=bl&ots=-
MjgRLp6hk&sig=VIUUDP3kTVmTU53kaRo9FQi8HDw&hl=en&ei=nh6MS4X5I
oSINOjSlW4&sa=X&oi=book_result&ct=result&resnum=7&ved=0CCQQ6AEw
Bg#v=onepage&q=&f=false

National Park Service; *Juan Bautista de Anza National Historic Trail Guide Imperial County CA)*; Internet publication available at http://www.solideas.com/DeAnza/TrailGuide/Imperial/index.html (accessed July 28, 2010)

Oregon - California Trails Association; *Learn. Connect. Preserve.*; Internet publication accessible at http://www.octa-trails.org/ (accessed October 9, 2010)

Ormsby, Waterman L.; *The Butterfield Overland Mail (Only Through Passenger on the First Westbound Stage)*; original publications New York Herald (NY) Sep 26 - Nov 19, 1858; republished by Henry E. Huntington Library and Art Gallery, San Marino CA, 1942 - 1998

Talbot, Don; *Historical Guide to the Mormon Battalion and Butterfield Trail;* Westernlore Press, 1992

Stage road, vicinity of Carrizo Creek station site (N32.878, W116.107.).
Photo by Fred Yeck (2006).

Carrizo Creek Station to Palm Springs Station
April 25, 2011

Carrizo Creek Station - Anza Borrego Desert State Park • San Diego County (N32° 52' 25.16", W116° 8' 17.23")

TO Palm Springs - Anza Borrego Desert State Park • San Diego County (N32° 54' 44.82", W116° 12' 19.12")

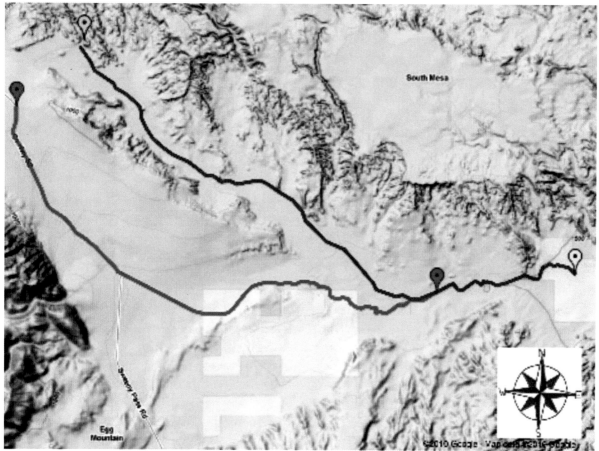

Approximate Actual Route Carrizo Creek to Palm Springs 8.2 miles.

(1858 Bailey itinerary says 9 miles)

Notes:

The Butterfield Route through this segment is within the Anza Borrego Desert State Park off of the main roads.

It continues to track the 1846-1847 Mormon Battalion route toward San Diego as well as the 1852 route used by John Russell Bartlett in his U.S. -

Mexico Boundary Survey and the 1857 course of the San Antonio - San Diego Stage route established by Skillman, Wasson, Birch et al.

It should also be noted that the Anza Borrego Desert State Park has taken steps to establish the Butterfield Route through the entire park as a recognized Cultural Preserve and should be closely consulted for cooperation during establishment of any National Trail or other Master Preservation Plan.

This segment continues along an essentially northwestward arc through the Anza Borrego Desert State Park.

The Palm Springs referred to in this report is **not** to be confused with the City of Palm Springs -- which is 60 miles north-northwest of this point in the Coachella Valley.

Palm Springs has been described by many pioneer travelers as a true oasis -- being a beautiful pool of water surrounded by native palm trees rather than the haunt of starlets and their wealthy squires.

Pages 469 - 470 of James' *The Wonders of the Colorado Desert* contain a somewhat overly-poetic description of the approach to the site of Palm Springs in the early 1900s, although he has little to say of the station itself.

Melissa Burton Couray, a member of the Mormon Battalion party, wrote of that group's arrival at Palm Springs on January 18, 1847, "The men were so used up from thirst, fatigue, and hunger there was no talking. Some could not speak at all; tongues were swollen and dark. Sixteen more mules gave out. Each man was down to his last four ounces of flour; there had been no sugar or coffee for weeks. Only five government wagons and three private wagons remained... When they arrived at Vallecito Creek, they rested and washed clothes and cleaned their guns. An Indian from a nearby village brought a letter from the alcalde in San Diego welcoming the Battalion to California. In the early evening there was singing and fiddling with a little dancing."

There is a California State Historical Marker near the site (#639) which reports "Palm Springs - Here Mexican pioneers coming to California between 1862 and 1866 rested among the palms, here, too, came mountain men, the Army of the West, the Mormon Battalion, a boundary commission, '49ers, a railway survey team, the Butterfield Overland Mail stages, and the California Legion. This was the site of the Butterfield stage station built in 1858 by Warren F. Hall."

Warren F. Hall was a Butterfield employee who had been hired specifically to locate and establish stations along the Overland Mail route. While the Carrizo Creek Station and Vallecito Station on either side of Palm Springs had been stops for the Birch line prior to Butterfield, Palm Springs Station was established specifically for the Butterfield.

Bailey and Ormsby (1858) both specifically mention Palm Springs. While Bartlett (1854) does not mention the locale in detail, he definitely would have traveled the area in his passage from Carrizo Creek to Vallecito.

Historic Spots in California reports that as of 1932, "… not even a palm is left to tell of the past." Talbot mentions Palm Springs in his recounting of the Mormon Battalion route and as a later Butterfield station.

The coordinates for this report (N32° 54' 44.82", W116° 12' 19.12") represent the nearest point one can reach to the Palm Springs Station site on navigable roads. In his correspondence of October 29, 2010, Chris Wray of the Oregon - California Trails Association states that their field research and mapping teams have identified the actual Palm Springs site approximately 1.25 miles due northeast of this point at coordinates N32° 55' 11.30", W116° 13' 9.53"

An additional resource for in-depth study of the Butterfield Route in Southern California during Planning and Implementation phases is the Wells Fargo Company Historical Museum (2733 San Diego Ave, San Diego CA).

References:

Bailey, Goddard; *California -- Arrival of the Overland Mail -- Itinerary of the Route*; as reported by newspaper article; New York Times (NY) - October 14, 1858

Bailey, Goddard; *Report to Postmaster General A.V. Brown - Full itinerary as reported by De Bow's Review and Industrial Resources, Statistics etc;* published by De Bow's Review; New Orleans and Washington City; 1858. See specifically *Internal Improvements - 1. Wagon Road to the Pacific;* pp 719-721. Internet accessible at http://books.google.com/books?id=5CYoAAAAYAAJ&pg=PA720&lpg=PA720&dq=Cienega+de+los+Pimas&source=bl&ots=_5lZw_Bq23&sig=T6scCb8cpbY7K wjxpYoNvZpcgvI&hl=en&ei=i6KnS6KNOIr2M5yprIED&sa=X&oi=book_result& ct=result&resnum=2&ved=0CAwQ6AEwAQ#v=onepage&q=Cienega%20de%20 los%20Pimas&f=false (accessed March 22, 2010)

Bartlett, John Russell; *Personal Narrative of Explorations and Incidents in Texas, New Mexico, California, Sonora and Chihuahua - Vol. One*; D. Appleton and Company; *New York; 1854*

California State Parks - Office of Historic Preservation; California Historical Landmarks; Internet database - http://www.parks.ca.gov/default.asp?page_id=21387 (accessed April 4, 2010)

Conkling, Roscoe P. and Margaret B.; *The Butterfield Overland Mail, 1857–1869* (3 vols); Glendale, CA: A. H.   Clark Company, 1947.

Hoover, Mildred Brooke, Hero Eugene Rensch and Ethel Grace Rensch; *Historic Spots in California*; Stanford University Press; Stanford CA; 1932 (rev 1948)

James, George Wharton; *The Wonders of the Colorado Desert (Southern California)*; Little, Brown & Company; Boston; 1906

Internet accessible at google books: http://books.google.com/books?id=clgTAAAAYAAJ&printsec=frontcover&dq=Wonders+of+the+colorado&source=bl&ots=-MjgRLp6hk&sig=VIUUDP3kTVmTU53kaRo9FQi8HDw&hl=en&ei=nh6MS4X5IoSINOjSlW4&sa=X&oi=book_result&ct=result&resnum=7&ved=0CCQQ6AEwBg#v=onepage&q=&f=false

Oregon - California Trails Association; *Learn. Connect. Preserve.*; Internet publication accessible at http://www.octa-trails.org/ (accessed October 9, 2010)

Ormsby, Waterman L.; *The Butterfield Overland Mail (Only Through Passenger on the First Westbound Stage)*; original publications New York Herald (NY) Sep 26 - Nov 19, 1858; republished by Henry E. Huntington Library and Art Gallery, San Marino CA, 1942 - 1998

Ricketts, Norma Baldwin; *Melissa's Journey With the Mormon Battalion: The Western Odyssey of Melissa Burton Couray, 1846-1848*; Salt Lake City: International Society Daughters of Utah Pioneers, 1984

Talbot, Don; *Historical Guide to the Mormon Battalion and Butterfield Trail;* Western Lore Press, 1992

Palm Springs Station to Vallecito Station
April 25, 2011

Palm Springs - Anza Borrego Desert State Park • **San Diego County** (N32° 54' 44.82", W116° 12' 19.12")

TO Vallecito Stage Station County Park - 37349 County Route S2 • **San Diego County** (N32° 58' 58.41", W116° 21' 24.80")

Approximate Actual Route Palm Springs to Vallecito 10 miles.

(1858 Bailey itinerary says 9 miles)

Notes:

Here again, the actual Butterfield Route meanders through the present-day Anza Borrego Desert State park. It continues to track the 1846-1847 Mormon Battalion route toward San Diego as well as the 1852 route used by John Russell Bartlett in his U.S. - Mexico Boundary Survey and the 1857 course of the San Antonio - San Diego Stage route established by Skillman, Wasson, Birch et al.

This segment continues along an essentially northwestward arc through the Anza Borrego Desert State Park.

San Diego County has established a park at the site of the Vallecito Station that includes a reproduction of the original Butterfield Station structure. The park was established in 1934 and is immediately adjacent to the Anza Borrego Desert State Park at coordinates N32° 58' 58.41", W116° 21' 24.80".

A brochure from the San Diego County Parks Department notes that "Countless generations of Native Americans camped here but left little evidence of their occupation. In contrast, a single generation of 19th Century Americans left indelible impressions. One example, the stage station, is testimony to the most dynamic decade of this area's history. First used as an army supply depot, then as a rest stop on the "Jackass Mail" between San Antonio and San Diego, the building was busiest during the lifetime of the Butterfield Overland Stage (1858 - 61). ... Stage stations scattered along the route offered the weary passengers a brief meal and rest as the horses were changed. Then it was on to the next stop on the 24-hour-a-day journey. Vallecito was a favorite such station, since it was the first place with greenery that travelers saw after crossing the hostile desert west of Yuma. But the Civil War ended the southern mail route, and Vallecito went into a slow decline."

The first recorded use of the Vallecito Station was by the Birch line's San Antonio-San Diego Mail. On August 31 of 1857, driver Isaiah Woods brought the first mail-bearing Birch coach safely into the station from Yuma, Arizona.

A California State Historical Marker stands at the location (#304); "Vallecito Stage Depot (Station) - A reconstruction (1934) of Vallecito Stage Station built in 1852 at the edge of the Great Colorado Desert. It was an important stop on the first official transcontinental route, serving the San Diego-San Antonio ('Jackass') mail line (1857 -1859), the Butterfield Overland Stage Line, and the southern emigrant caravans."

It is fortunate that San Diego County has reproduced and preserved the Vallecito Station site. *Historic Spots in California* (first published two years before the county's acquisition of the site) reports "Vallecito has long been deserted, a prey to vandals and earthquakes, its walls, built of sod, rapidly crumbling before the elements. Nearby are a number of graves and the one gravestone in the place records the death of one 'John Hart at the age of 30 years in the year 1867.'"

Ormsby and Bailey both specifically mention the Vallecito Station. Couray describes the movement of the Mormon Battalion through the vicinity of Vallecito. Bartlett also discusses having camped at "Vallecita" in the early 1850s. James wrote of having visited the "Vallecita" area circa 1906. Talbot also mentions Vallecito in conjunction with both the Mormon Battalion and as a Butterfield Station. Ruth Pittman also discusses the Vallecito Stage Station Park in her *Roadside History of California*.

References:

Bailey, Goddard; *California -- Arrival of the Overland Mail -- Itinerary of the Route*; as reported by newspaper article; New York Times (NY) - October 14, 1858

Bailey, Goddard; *Report to Postmaster General A.V. Brown - Full itinerary as reported by De Bow's Review and Industrial Resources, Statistics etc;* published by De Bow's Review; New Orleans and Washington City; 1858. See specifically *Internal Improvements - 1. Wagon Road to the Pacific*; pp 719-721. Internet accessible at http://books.google.com/books?id=5CYoAAAAYAAJ&pg=PA720&lpg=PA720& dq=Cienega+de+los+Pimas&source=bl&ots=_5lZw_Bq23&sig=T6scCb8cpbY7K wjxpYoNvZpcgvI&hl=en&ei=i6KnS6KNOIr2M5yprIED&sa=X&oi=book_result& ct=result&resnum=2&ved=0CAwQ6AEwAQ#v=onepage&q=Cienega%20de%20 los%20Pimas&f=false (accessed March 22, 2010)

Bartlett, John Russell; *Personal Narrative of Explorations and Incidents in Texas, New Mexico, California, Sonora and Chihuahua - Vol. One*; D. Appleton and Company; *New York; 1854*

California State Parks - Office of Historic Preservation; California Historical Landmarks; Internet database - http://www.parks.ca.gov/default.asp?page_id=21387 (accessed April 4, 2010)

Conkling, Roscoe P. and Margaret B.; *The Butterfield Overland Mail, 1857–1869* (3 vols); Glendale, CA: A. H. Clark Company, 1947.

Hoover, Mildred Brooke, Hero Eugene Rensch and Ethel Grace Rensch; *Historic Spots in California*; Stanford University Press; Stanford CA; 1932 (rev 1948)

James, George Wharton; *The Wonders of the Colorado Desert (Southern California)*; Little, Brown & Company; Boston; 1906

Internet accessible at google books:
http://books.google.com/books?id=clgTAAAAYAAJ&printsec=frontcover&dq=Wonders+of+the+colorado&source=bl&ots=-MjgRLp6hk&sig=VIUUDP3kTVmTU53kaRo9FQi8HDw&hl=en&ei=nh6MS4X5IoSINOjSlW4&sa=X&oi=book_result&ct=result&resnum=7&ved=0CCQQ6AEwBg#v=onepage&q=&f=false

Ormsby, Waterman L.; *The Butterfield Overland Mail (Only Through Passenger on the First Westbound Stage)*; original publications New York Herald (NY) Sep 26 - Nov 19, 1858; republished by Henry E. Huntington Library and Art Gallery, San Marino CA, 1942 - 1998

Oregon - California Trails Association; *Learn. Connect. Preserve.*; Internet publication accessible at http://www.octa-trails.org/ (accessed October 9, 2010)

Pittman, Ruth; *Roadside History of California*; Mountain Press Publishing; Missoula MT; 1995

Ricketts, Norma Baldwin; *Melissa's Journey With the Mormon Battalion: The Western Odyssey of Melissa Burton Couray, 1846-1848*; Salt Lake City: International Society Daughters of Utah Pioneers, 1984

San Diego (County of) Parks Department; *Vallecito County Park*; brochure; Internet accessible at http://www.co.san-diego.ca.us/parks/Camping/vallecito.html

Talbot, Don; *Historical Guide to the Mormon Battalion and Butterfield Trail;* Westernlore Press, 1992

Vallecito Station to San Felipe Station
April 24, 2011

Vallecito Stage Station County Park - 37349 County Route • San Diego County (N32° 58' 58.41", W116° 21' 24.80")

TO San Felipe Station (approximate) - near Banner • San Diego County (N33° 06' 06.72", W116° 29' 03.63")

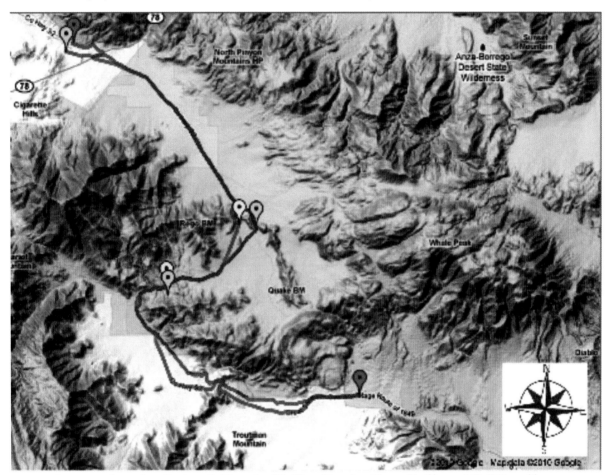

Approximate Actual Route Vallecito to San Felipe 18.25 miles.

(1858 Bailey itinerary says 18 miles)

Secondary Landmarks:

Box Canyon (Cooke's Pass) Historical Marker per Wray - Anza Borrego Desert State Park - coordinates N33° 00' 55.41", W116° 26' 35.69"

Box Canyon Vicinity per Wray - Anza Borrego Desert State Park - coordinates N33° 00' 43.24, W116° 26' 33.14"

Blair Valley (Auto Tour) - Anza Borrego Desert State Park - approximate coordinates N33° 02' 14.14", W116° 24' 39.07"

Blair Valley Actual (Little Pass) per Wray - Anza Borrego Desert State Park - coordinates N33° 00' 43.24, W116° 26' 33.14"

Notes:

Here again, the Butterfield Route meanders through the present-day Anza Borrego Desert State Park.

It continues to track the 1846-1847 Mormon Battalion route toward San Diego as well as the 1852 route used by John Russell Bartlett in his U.S. - Mexico Boundary Survey and the 1857 course of the San Antonio - San Diego Stage route established by Skillman, Wasson, Birch et al.

Once again, the actual Butterfield Route as measured by Anza Borrego Park personnel and the Oregon - California Trails Association research teams roughly tracks (but diverges slightly from) County Road S2.

There are two intermediate locations of note on this section of the route. The first was the site of a tale of hardships overcome against incredible odds. The second brought great sighs of relief to travelers through the area.

In January of 1847, the wagon train of the Mormon Battalion emigrants reached what they referred to as Box Canyon. As the advance party made its way through the small canyon, they discovered that the canyon thinned as it progressed and the party was faced with a trail through which their wagons were too wide to pass.

Further, the advance party had lost a wagon bearing most of its tools in a difficult crossing of the Colorado River at Yuma. With grit, determination and perhaps a healthy dose of desperation, they hacked out the walls of the canyon with little more than axes and a crowbar so that their wagons could pass.

In the words of Daniel Tyler, a member and chronicler of the Battalion's journey, "As we traveled up the dry bed, the chasm became more contracted until we found ourselves in a passage at least a foot narrower than our wagons. Nearly all of our road tools, such as picks, shovels, spades, etc., had been lost in the boat disaster [at Yuma Crossing]. The principal ones remaining were a few axes ... a small crow bar, and perhaps a spade or two. These were brought into requisition, the commander taking an ax and assisting the pioneers. Considerable was done before the wagons arrived... The passage was hewn out and the remaining wagons got through about sundown, by unloading and lifting through all but two light ones, which were hauled by the mules."

A California Historical Site Marker near the canyon (#472, Box Canyon) reports "The old road, known as the Sonora, Colorado River, or Southern Emigrant Trail and later as the Butterfield Overland Mail Route, traversed Box Canyon just east of here. On January 19, 1847, the Mormon Battalion under the command of Lieutenant Colonel Philip St. G. Cooke, using hand tools, hewed a passage through the rocky walls of the narrow gorge for their wagons and opened the first road into Southern California."

When surveyors and engineers for the Butterfield came through the area in 1857, they widened the earlier Box Canyon Pass so that it would accommodate larger coaches and wagons. Thereafter, "Box Canyon" was also referred to as "Cooke's Pass" in honor of Philip Saint George Cooke, one of the leaders of the Mormon Battalion expedition.

In correspondence as of October 29, 2010, Wray identified the site of this marker at coordinates N33° 00' 55.41", W116° 26' 35.69"

The next location is a much more pleasant story, marking the point at which the Colorado Desert begins to merge with greener lands beyond. Blair Valley is marked as California Historical site #647 Butterfield Overland Mail Route "This pass, Puerta, between the desert and the cooler valleys to the north, was used by the Mormon Battalion, Kearny's Army of the West, the Butterfield Overland Mail stages, and emigrants who eventually settled the West. The eroded scar on the left was the route of the Butterfield stages, 1858-1861. The road on the right served as a county road until recent years" Blair Valley marker approximate coordinates are N33° 02' 14.14", W116° 24' 39.07".

Wray reports that the actual Butterfield Route entered Blair Valley at a point referred to as "Little Pass" approximately 0.5 mile east of this location (coordinates N33° 00' 43.24, W116° 26' 33.14")

Box Canyon and Blair Valley are both within the Anza Borrego Desert State Park.

The San Felipe Station (approximate coordinates N33° 06' 06.72", W116° 29' 03.63") was established by Warren F. Hall. An historical marker in the vicinity (California Historical Site marker #793 San Felipe Valley Stage Station) notes that "Here the southern trail of explorers, trappers, soldiers, and emigrants crossed ancient trade routes of Kamia, Cahuilla, Diegueño, and Luiseño Indians. On the flat southwest across the creek, Warren F. Hall built and operated the San Felipe home station of the Butterfield Mail, which operated from 1858 to 1861. Later the station was used by Banning Stages and by the military during the Civil War."

Wray reports the actual station site as being off-road approximately 1500 feet due southwest of these coordinates at N33° 05' 56.20, W116° 29' 15.18".

Bartlett places San Felipe as being eighteen miles from Vallecito (as does Bailey). Pittman discusses Box Canyon and the San Felipe Station. Ormsby mentions Box Canyon and San Felipe Station. Bailey specifically notes San Felipe Station as a mileage point. James writes in some depth about this segment of the route. Hoover also mentions Box Canyon and the area in general.

Of the route through this area in general, Wray notes that the actual Butterfield Route seldom traveled directly upon what is now designated as County Highway S2 / Great Southern Overland Mail Route of 1849 but for "a few feet at a stretch". Rather, the trail meandered through the washes in the Anza Borrego Desert State Park in the general vicinity of Highway S2. Both Wray and the Anza Borrego State Park personnel have detailed measurements of the historical route through the park.

References:

Bailey, Goddard; *California -- Arrival of the Overland Mail -- Itinerary of the Route*; as reported by newspaper article; New York Times (NY) - October 14, 1858

Bailey, Goddard; *Report to Postmaster General A.V. Brown - Full itinerary as reported by De Bow's Review and Industrial Resources, Statistics etc;* published by De Bow's Review; New Orleans and Washington City; 1858. See specifically *Internal Improvements - 1. Wagon Road to the Pacific;* pp 719-721. Internet accessible at http://books.google.com/books?id=5CYoAAAAYAAJ&pg=PA720&lpg=PA720& dq=Cienega+de+los+Pimas&source=bl&ots=_5lZw_Bq23&sig=T6scCb8cpbY7K wjxpYoNvZpcgvI&hl=en&ei=i6KnS6KNOIr2M5yprIED&sa=X&oi=book_result& ct=result&resnum=2&ved=0CAwQ6AEwAQ#v=onepage&q=Cienega%20de%20 los%20Pimas&f=false (accessed March 22, 2010)

Bartlett, John Russell; *Personal Narrative of Explorations and Incidents in Texas, New Mexico, California, Sonora and Chihuahua - Vol. One*; D. Appleton and Company; *New York; 1854*

California State Parks - Office of Historic Preservation; California Historical Landmarks; Internet database - http://www.parks.ca.gov/default.asp?page_id=21387 (accessed April 4, 2010)

Conkling, Roscoe P. and Margaret B.; *The Butterfield Overland Mail, 1857–1869* (Three Volumes); Glendale, CA: A. H. Clark Company, 1947.

Hoover, Mildred Brooke, Hero Eugene Rensch and Ethel Grace Rensch; *Historic Spots in California*; Stanford University Press; Stanford CA; 1932 (rev 1948)

James, George Wharton; *The Wonders of the Colorado Desert (Southern California)*; Little, Brown & Company; Boston; 1906

Internet accessible at Google Books:
http://books.google.com/books?id=clgTAAAAYAAJ&printsec=frontcover&dq=Wonders+of+the+colorado&source=bl&ots=-MjgRLp6hk&sig=VIUUDP3kTVmTU53kaRo9FQi8HDw&hl=en&ei=nh6MS4X5IoSINOjSlW4&sa=X&oi=book_result&ct=result&resnum=7&ved=0CCQQ6AEwBg#v=onepage&q=&f=false

Oregon - California Trails Association; *Learn. Connect. Preserve.*; Internet publication accessible at http://www.octa-trails.org/ (accessed October 9, 2010)

Ormsby, Waterman L.; *The Butterfield Overland Mail (Only Through Passenger on the First Westbound Stage)*; original publications New York Herald (NY) Sep 26 - Nov 19, 1858; republished by Henry E. Huntington Library and Art Gallery, San Marino CA, 1942 - 1998

Pittman, Ruth; *Roadside History of California*; Mountain Press Publishing; Missoula MT; 1995

Tyler, Daniel; *A Concise History of the Mormon Battalion in the Mexican War 1846 - 1847*; unknown publisher; 1881; also accessible on Internet at http://books.google.com/books?id=XdUBAAAAMAAJ&printsec=frontcover&dq=Daniel+Tyler+Mormon+Battalion&source=bl&ots=KSliN5gUtI&sig=cDXlTOtqscCdobXMu22RmrFBA8s&hl=en&ei=5mICTJ2WO6TKM-vT2Ts&sa=X&oi=book_result&ct=result#v=onepage&q&f=false

San Felipe Station to Warner Ranch
April 24, 2011

San Felipe Station - near Banner • San Diego County (N33° 06' 06.72", W116° 29' 03.63")

TO Warner Ranch - se of Warner Springs • San Diego County (N33° 14' 32.13", W116° 39' 57.03")

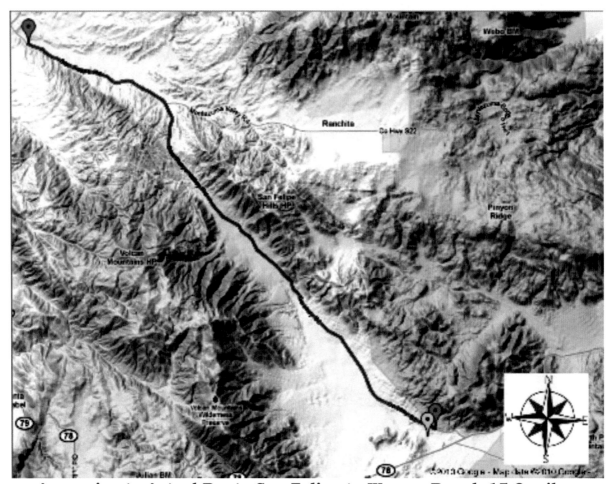

Approximate Actual Route San Felipe to Warner Ranch 15.2 miles.

(1858 Bailey itinerary says 16 miles)

Notes:

The historical route followed by Butterfield through this segment continues to track the 1846-1847 Mormon Battalion route toward San Diego as well as the 1852 route used by John Russell Bartlett in his U.S. - Mexico Boundary Survey and the 1857 course of the San Antonio - San Diego Stage route established by Skillman, Wasson, Birch et al.

The modern San Felipe Valley Road closely approximates the actual route used by the Butterfield coaches. While the original route may have deviated slightly from the modern road, it appears that any such deviations were within a few feet of the existing roadway.

The next station is one of a very few where an original Butterfield-era structure still stands, although recent reports indicate the structures at Warner Ranch are in need of repair and restoration.

Warner Ranch was a well-known stop for travelers for at least a decade prior to the Butterfield's arrival. Jonathan Trumbull Warner, a trapper and trader from Connecticut who had come to California in 1833, took Mexican citizenship and was given a substantial land grant in this area in 1844.

Pittman notes that "As the first bit of civilization west of the Colorado Desert, Warner Ranch became a famous way-station for all who entered the state over the Emigrant Trail from Yuma. In 1846, Kearny and his dragoons sought refuge there on a night before the Battle at San Pasqual. The next year, Warner provided a stopover point for the Mormon Battalion on their march from Santa Fe to San Diego. Later still, the ranch became a stop on the Butterfield Stage Route, with the first coach arriving on October 6, 1858."

California Historical Site Marker #311 stands at the Warner Ranch home site near the Butterfield structure (coordinates N33° 14' 32.13", W116° 39' 57.03"). It reads "In 1844, Governor Manuel Micheltorena granted 44,322 acres to Juan José Warner, who built this house. General Kearny passed here in 1846, and the Mormon Battalion in 1847. The first Butterfield Stage stopped at this ranch on October 6, 1858, on its 2,600-mile, 24-day trip from Tipton, Missouri to San Francisco, the southern overland route into California." Warner Ranch is listed on the National Register of Historic Places (1966 - #66000228).

Recent information from the National Historic Landmarks Program lists the Warner homesite as "... limited public access. Improved but still threatened. (2004) The adobe ranch house is in very deteriorated condition and in danger of collapse. The porch floor and a portion of the front wall already have collapsed. Exposed portions of the adobe walls are eroding. Repairs with incompatible materials have accelerated rising damp and have caused further erosion of the adobe. The barn has also suffered damage, and the walls are failing."

• Data update as of April 2013, Fred Yeck reports that "Just last month I stopped at the Warner Ranch Station in California. This station has been beautifully restored and is now open to the public for guided tours, including the old Butterfield barn which has been stabilized and will be restored."

Ormsby and Bailey both specifically mention Warner Ranch. James' discussion of Warner Ranch contains two hand-drawn sketches of the facility. Hoover writes in some detail of Warner Ranch in general and as a Butterfield Station. Tyler also mentions Warner Ranch in connection with the activities of the Mormon Battalion.

Wray's data according to the Oregon - California Trails Association team research confirms this site.

References:

Bailey, Goddard; *California -- Arrival of the Overland Mail -- Itinerary of the Route*; as reported by newspaper article; New York Times (NY) - October 14, 1858

Bailey, Goddard; *Report to Postmaster General A.V. Brown - Full itinerary as reported by De Bow's Review and Industrial Resources, Statistics etc;* published by De Bow's Review; New Orleans and Washington City; 1858. See specifically *Internal Improvements - 1. Wagon Road to the Pacific*; pp 719-721. Internet accessible at http://books.google.com/books?id=5CYoAAAAYAAJ&pg=PA720&lpg=PA720& dq=Cienega+de+los+Pimas&source=bl&ots=_5lZw_Bq23&sig=T6scCb8cpbY7K wjxpYoNvZpcgvI&hl=en&ei=i6KnS6KNOIr2M5yprIED&sa=X&oi=book_result& ct=result&resnum=2&ved=0CAwQ6AEwAQ#v=onepage&q=Cienega%20de%20 los%20Pimas&f=false (accessed March 22, 2010)

Conkling, Roscoe P. and Margaret B.; *The Butterfield Overland Mail, 1857–1869* (3 vols); Glendale, CA: A. H. Clark Company, 1947.

Hoover, Mildred Brooke, Hero Eugene Rensch and Ethel Grace Rensch; *Historic Spots in California*; Stanford University Press; Stanford CA; 1932 (rev 1948)

James, George Wharton; *The Wonders of the Colorado Desert (Southern California)*; Little, Brown & Company; Boston; 1906

Internet accessible at google books:
http://books.google.com/books?id=clgTAAAAYAAJ&printsec=frontcover&dq= Wonders+of+the+colorado&source=bl&ots=-MjgRLp6hk&sig=VIUUDP3kTVmTU53kaRo9FQi8HDw&hl=en&ei=nh6MS4X5I oSINOjSlW4&sa=X&oi=book_result&ct=result&resnum=7&ved=0CCQQ6AEw Bg#v=onepage&q=&f=false

National Park Service; *Warner Ranch*; National Historic Landmarks Program; Internet accessible at
http://tps.cr.nps.gov/nhl/detail.cfm?ResourceId=132&ResourceType=Buildi ng

Oregon - California Trails Association; *Learn. Connect. Preserve.*; Internet publication accessible at http://www.octa-trails.org/ (accessed October 9, 2010)

Ormsby, Waterman L.; *The Butterfield Overland Mail (Only Through Passenger on the First Westbound Stage)*; original publications New York Herald (NY) Sep 26 - Nov 19, 1858; republished by Henry E. Huntington Library and Art Gallery, San Marino CA, 1942 - 1998

Pittman, Ruth; *Roadside History of California*; Mountain Press Publishing; Missoula MT; 1995

Tyler, Daniel; *A Concise History of the Mormon Battalion in the Mexican War 1846 - 1847*; unknown publisher; 1881; also accessible on Internet at
http://books.google.com/books?id=XdUBAAAAMAAJ&printsec=frontcover&d q=Daniel+Tyler+Mormon+Battalion&source=bl&ots=KSliN5gUtI&sig=cDXlTOt qscCdobXMu22RmrFBA8s&hl=en&ei=5mICTJ2WO6TKM-vT2Ts&sa=X&oi=book_result&ct=result#v=onepage&q&f=false

Warner Ranch to Oak Grove Station
April 25, 2011

Warner Ranch - southwest of Warner Springs • San Diego County (N33° 14' 32.13", W116° 39' 57.03")

TO Oak Grove • San Diego County (N33° 23' 25.08", W116° 47' 40.92")

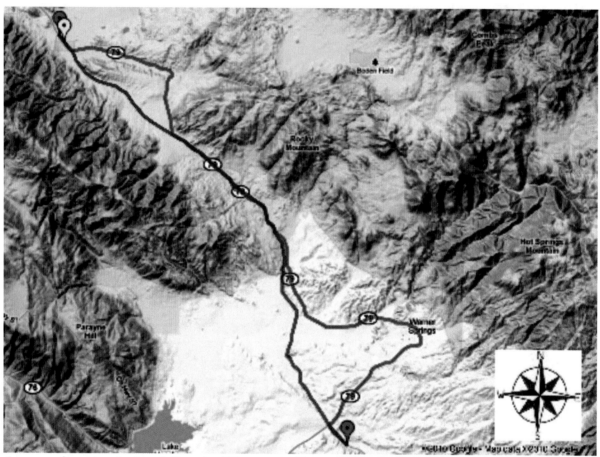

Approximate Actual Route Warner's Ranch to Oak Grove 13.75 miles.

(1858 Bailey itinerary says 10 miles)

Secondary Landmarks:

Camp Wright Historical Marker - coordinates N33° 23' 15.82", W116° 47' 34.85"

Notes:

The Butterfield Route through this segment diverges from the main 1846-1847 Mormon Battalion route toward San Diego, the 1852 route used by John Russell Bartlett in his U.S. - Mexico Boundary Survey and the 1857 course of the San Antonio - San Diego Stageline established by Skillman, Wasson, Birch et al.

Warner Ranch was located at the intersection of two early trails, one leading southwesterly toward San Diego and the other continuing northwesterly toward Los Angeles. The Mormon Battalion, Bartlett and the San Antonio - San Diego Stage route took the southwesterly trail while the Butterfield continued along the northwesterly route.

While the original Butterfield Route through this segment appears to follow within proximity of the modern road for the most part, the modern road meanders somewhat -- adding several unnecessary miles to a fairly straight-forward valley route.

The original route, given Bailey's mileage figure and terrain, appears to have followed the valley to the west of (and bypassing) the modern town of Warner Springs, joining what is now California Highway 79 near the southeastern foot of Palomar Mountain and continuing between the foothills of Palomar and Rocky mountains. At the northern end of the foothills pass, the original route appears to have continued northwesterly to the southwest of California Highway 79 -- skirting Palomar Mountain, whereas the modern highway trims to the north and then west at the northwestern tip of Rocky Mountain.

No specific research has been found to-date that would more exactly pinpoint this route. For lack of identified local expertise on this segment, additional field research is needed.

Oak Grove Station (California Historic Site Marker #502) is another location where the original Butterfield building still stands and is readily located at coordinates N33° 23' 25.08", W116° 47' 40.92". The marker notes "Oak Grove is one of the few remaining stations on the Butterfield Overland Mail route, which operated between San Francisco and two eastern terminals-Saint Louis, Missouri and Memphis, Tennessee-from September

15, 1858 to March 2, 1861. During the Civil War the station was used as a hospital for nearby Camp Wright."

The Oak Grove Butterfield Station is listed on the National Register of Historic Places (1966 - #66000222).

In correspondence dated November 7, 2010, local historian Phil Brigandi reported that only a portion of the current Oak Grove Station structure is original Butterfield. He also noted that "So far as I know, it is the only original Butterfield station built by the company still standing in Southern California."

There is another historical marker nearby commemorating the service of the Warner Ranch area as Camp Wright during the Civil War (coordinates N33° 23' 15.82", W116° 47' 34.85".

The nearby historical site marker for the Civil War era Camp Wright California Historic Site Marker #482) reads "Camp Wright, named for Brigadier General George Wright, United States Army, who commanded the Pacific Department and California District from 1861 to 1865, was first established October 18, 1861 on Warner's Ranch to guard the line of communication between California and Arizona. The camp was moved to this site by Major Edwin A. Rigg, First California Volunteers, about November 23, 1861 and was abandoned December 1866."

Ormsby mentions this station as "Hall's Oak Grove". Bailey mentions Oak Grove specifically as a mileage point. James mentions the Oak Grove Station and includes a hand-drawn sketch of the structure.

References:

Bailey, Goddard; *California -- Arrival of the Overland Mail -- Itinerary of the Route*; as reported by newspaper article; New York Times (NY) - October 14, 1858

Bailey, Goddard; *Report to Postmaster General A.V. Brown - Full itinerary as reported by De Bow's Review and Industrial Resources, Statistics etc*; published by De Bow's Review; New Orleans and Washington City; 1858. See specifically *Internal Improvements - 1. Wagon Road to the Pacific*; pp 719-721. Internet accessible at http://books.google.com/books?id=5CYoAAAAYAAJ&pg=PA720&lpg=PA720&dq=Cienega+de+los+Pimas&source=bl&ots=_5lZw_Bq23&sig=T6scCb8cpbY7K wjxpYoNvZpcgvI&hl=en&ei=i6KnS6KNOIr2M5yprIED&sa=X&oi=book_result&

ct=result&resnum=2&ved=0CAwQ6AEwAQ#v=onepage&q=Cienega%20de%20
los%20Pimas&f=false (accessed March 22, 2010)

California (State of); *State Historical Markers (San Diego County)*; database
internet accessible at
http://ceres.ca.gov/geo_area/counties/San_Diego/landmarks.html

Conkling, Roscoe P. and Margaret B.; *The Butterfield Overland Mail, 1857–
1869* (3 vols); Glendale, CA: A. H. Clark Company, 1947.

James, George Wharton; *The Wonders of the Colorado Desert (Southern
California)*; Little, Brown & Company; Boston; 1906

Internet accessible at Google Books:
http://books.google.com/books?id=clgTAAAAYAAJ&printsec=frontcover&dq=
Wonders+of+the+colorado&source=bl&ots=-
MjgRLp6hk&sig=VIUUDP3kTVmTU53kaRo9FQi8HDw&hl=en&ei=nh6MS4X5I
oSINOjSlW4&sa=X&oi=book_result&ct=result&resnum=7&ved=0CCQQ6AEw
Bg#v=onepage&q=&f=false

National Park Service; *Oak Grove Butterfield Station*; National Historic
Landmarks Program; Internet accessible at
http://tps.cr.nps.gov/nhl/detail.cfm?ResourceId=127&ResourceType=Buildi
ng

National Register of Historic Places; *National Register Locations by State*;
Internet publication; accessible at

http://www.nationalregisterofhistoricplaces.com/state.html (accessed May 3,
2010)

Ormsby, Waterman L.; *The Butterfield Overland Mail (Only Through
Passenger on the First Westbound Stage)*; original publications New York
Herald (NY) Sep 26 - Nov 19, 1858; republished by Henry E. Huntington
Library and Art Gallery, San Marino CA, 1942 - 1998

Oak Grove Station to Aguanga, California
April 25, 2011

Oak Grove • San Diego County (N33° 23' 25.08", W116° 47' 40.92")

TO Aguanga • Riverside County (N33° 26' 54.06", W116° 53' 28.86"

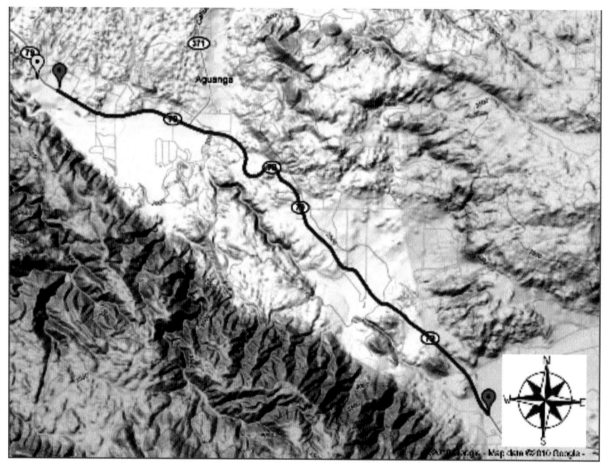

Approximate Actual Route Oak Grove to Aguanga 7.6 miles.

(1858 Bailey itinerary says 12 miles)

Secondary Landmarks:

Stagecoach Inn - 43851 California Highway 79 - coordinates N33° 26' 54.06", W116° 53' 28.86"

Notes:

As in the previous segment report, the original Butterfield Route through this segment is not well documented. Given the terrain, however, there are few options for passage other than what remains as the modern route of California Highway 79. Any divergence between the modern highway and the Butterfield Route would have been a matter of feet or yards.

While additional field research through this segment is advisable, it would be surprising to discover data that indicated any course substantially different from that of California Highway 79.

In the case of the next Butterfield Station, it appears that local reports may be more accurate in locating this station than were the early published reports.

Bailey's reports show the station between Oak Grove and Temecula to be "Tejungo." Ormsby referred to it as "Swango." Several researchers over the years have mimicked Bailey and Ormsby by reciting these same station names. Unfortunately, the nearest locales to this area with any such name (historical or current) would be Tujunga, California --near Los Angeles and 105 miles northwest -- or the town of Tejungo in Mozambique, Africa. "Swango" most commonly refers to a hybrid style of dancing that combines swing jazz and tango and cannot be found as a place name in California (or anywhere else, for that matter).

The etymology of the term "Tujunga / Tejungo" doesn't help much either. In the California native dialects it generally comes from the Temeku / Luiseño Indian term "tuyunga," meaning "mountain range" or from "tu'xuu" meaning "old woman" compounded to "tu'xuunga" meaning "place of the old woman." In which case, most any mountain range could have been referred to as a "tejungo" -- especially if an old woman lived nearby.

It would appear that Ormsby's and Bailey's Anglo-European ears may have misheard the local Luiseño Indian name "Aguanga" (land of water) as "Tejungo" and "Swango" given that the mileages cited in their itineraries would place "Tejungo / Swango" in reasonable proximity to an early Luiseño settlement that retains the name of Aguanga.

In correspondence dated November 7, 2010, local historian Phil Brigandi reported that the name Aguanga "... apparently refers to the spring where the Butterfield station was later built ..." and that the name Aguanga "...means *water that bubbles up out of the ground*. It appears (with the current spelling) in mission records as early as 1807."

Local research places a Butterfield station near the current site of the Stagecoach Inn cafe at 43851 California Highway 79 two miles west of Aguanga (coordinates N33° 26' 54.06", W116° 53' 28.86").

Additional research by the E Clampus Vitus historical / fraternal society concurs. A marker of theirs set near the Stagecoach Inn site (Caprice Road and California Highway 79; approximate coordinates N33° 26' 54.06", W116° 53' 28.86") recognizes "Jacob Bergman 1832-1869 -- Gracious Host; Station Keeper; Stage Driver; U.S. Trooper; "A House Beside the Road - A Friend to Man."

Some sources indicate that Jacob Bergman and Warren Hall (who operated the Oak Grove Station) were both employed by the Butterfield Overland Mail and crewed the first Fort Yuma to Temecula run in September 1858.

Brigandi, however, disputes the idea that Bergman was a Butterfield employee, stating that "Jake Bergman was not a driver for the Butterfield. He was still serving in the Army at that time, and did not come to Aguanga until about 1864. He worked with the Star Route [postal] stages in the 1870s. It was his grandson, Harry Bergman, who perpetuated the myth that he was a Butterfield driver. 'It wasn't that he was lying,' Harry's sister-in-law once said to me, 'he was just trying to make things interesting.'"

Brigandi does note specifically, however, that the Aguanga Station "...was located near the base of the hills, a little southwest of [the E Clampus Vitus marker]. The lines of the adobe walls were still quite evident the last time I was there, and a wooden addition, built by the Bergmans in the 1870s or '80s still stands. ... The site is on private property, and not currently accessible. The little Bergman family cemetery is across the highway [from the original Aguanga Station site] and still owned by the family, who continue to live in the area."

For the purpose of this report, we have used the coordinates of the Bergman marker as the reference point. This is not to discount the significance of the Stagecoach Inn location (0.3 mile northwest of the Bergman marker). Rather, it is to call attention to a significant but easily overlooked historical marker. This placement (regardless of a direct Jacob

Bergman connection to the Butterfield), can also be readily balanced to Brigandi's citation of the Butterfield Station as "... located near the base of the hills, a little southwest of [the E Clampus Vitus marker] ... across the highway [from the Bergman Cemetery]."

Hoover, Rensch and Rensch in *Historical Spots In California (1948)* also note, "The old Emigrant Trail, which followed Anza's route across the Colorado Desert as far as Carrizo Creek and crossed the mountains via Warner's Ranch, branched in two directions after leaving Aguanga; one branch, known as the San Bernardino - Sonora Road, traveled north to San Gorgonio Pass and west through the San Bernardino Valley, while the other, known in Mission Days as the Canyon Road to the Colorado and designated by the Los Angeles Court of Session, May 19,1851, as the Colorado Road took its course along the western mountains via Temecula, Elsinore, Temescal Canyon, Corona and the Santa Ana River."

The Butterfield route through this segment appears to have followed the "Colorado Road" (rejoining the earlier de Anza Anza Route) and would certainly have passed the Bergman / Stagecoach Inn sites; however, little additional information could be found regarding the Aguanga / Tejungo /Swango Station. No substantial remains of the original station appear to have been definitively documented.

References:

Bailey, Goddard; *California -- Arrival of the Overland Mail -- Itinerary of the Route*; as reported by newspaper article; New York Times (NY) - October 14, 1858

Bailey, Goddard; *Report to Postmaster General A.V. Brown - Full itinerary as reported by De Bow's Review and Industrial Resources, Statistics etc;* published by De Bow's Review; New Orleans and Washington City; 1858. See specifically *Internal Improvements - 1. Wagon Road to the Pacific;* pp 719-721. Internet accessible at http://books.google.com/books?id=5CYoAAAAYAAJ&pg=PA720&lpg=PA720&dq=Cienega+de+los+Pimas&source=bl&ots=_5lZw_Bq23&sig=T6scCb8cpbY7KwjxpYoNvZpcgvI&hl=en&ei=i6KnS6KNOIr2M5yprIED&sa=X&oi=book_result&ct=result&resnum=2&ved=0CAwQ6AEwAQ#v=onepage&q=Cienega%20de%20los%20Pimas&f=false (accessed March 22, 2010)

Conkling, Roscoe P. and Margaret B.; *The Butterfield Overland Mail, 1857–1869* (3 vols); Glendale, CA: A. H. Clarke Company, 1947.

E Clampus Vitus Society - *Billy Holcomb Chapter Plaques; Jacob Bergman Gravesite*; Internet accessible at http://www.billyholcomb.com/billy_holcomb_chapter_plaques.htm and http://www.billyholcomb.com/Bergman.jpg (accessed May 31, 2010)

Ormsby, Waterman L.; *The Butterfield Overland Mail (Only Through Passenger on the First Westbound Stage)*; original publications New York Herald (NY) Sep 26 - Nov 19, 1858; republished by Henry E. Huntington Library and Art Gallery, San Marino CA, 1942 – 1998

Jacob Bergman historical marker, Aguanga CA (N33° 26.902, W116° 53.481). Photo by Michael Kindig (2010). Courtesy of E Clampus Vitus Society - Billy Holcomb Chapter.

Aguanga, California to Temecula, California

February 26,2012

Aguanga • Riverside County (N33° 26' 54.06", W116° 53' 28.86"

TO Temecula (Redhawk Community Park) • Riverside County
(N33° 28' 34.06", W117° 5' 58.80")

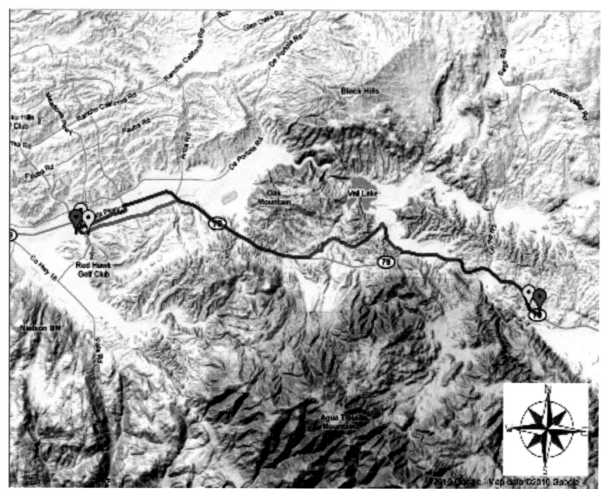

Approximate Actual Route Aguanga to Temecula 14.5 miles.

(1858 Bailey itinerary says 14 miles)

Secondary Landmarks:

Stagecoach Inn - 43851 California Highway 79; Aguanga CA - coordinates N33° 26' 54.06", W116° 53' 28.86"

Radec CA (landmark only) - coordinates N33° 27' 51.11", W116° 54' 50.09"

Wolf's Store - N33° 28' 45.48", W117° 5' 52.08"

Magee's Store - Linalou Ranch Road / Redhawk Parkway near Overland Trail - N33° 28' 32.88", W117° 5' 40.20"

Notes:

The Butterfield Route through this segment appears to have followed California Highway 79 to a great extent.

In correspondence as of November 7, 2010, local historian Phil Brigandi states that the Butterfield Route from Aguanga to Temecula diverged slightly from a straight follow of California Highway 79. Says Brigandi, "It apparently branched off closer to the little crossroads community of Radec ... we now know that the old emigrant road left the route of Highway 79 and made a dogleg north to about where Vail Lake is today."

This divergence indicates a route to the west from Radec CA (coordinates N33° 27' 51.11", W116° 54' 50.09") along California Highway 79 for approximately 2.5 miles to Vail Oak Road (coordinates N33° 28' 12.49", W116° 57' 12.53"). At this point, the Butterfield essentially tracked Vail Oak Road northwardly toward Vail Lake. At the northern foot of Agua Tibia Mountain, the route then dropped southwesterly through a pass that skirts between Agua Tibia and Oak Mountain (still following modern Vail Oak Road) to a point where it rejoins the course of California Highway 79 (coordinates N33° 28' 5.52", W116° 59' 52.57").

The Butterfield Route then continues to track the modern course of California Highway 79 to the eastern edge of the modern city of Temecula near the intersection of CA-79 and Anza Road (coordinates N33° 29' 16.04", W117° 3' 9.51").

At that point, according to local research, the Butterfield tracked "off-road" along the south bank of Temecula Creek whereas the course of CA-79 follows the north bank of the creek.

According to most scholars, the location of the original village of Temecula -- and therefore the Temecula Station of the Butterfield -- was slightly southeast of the present town of Temecula. The original landholding in what would become the stage station area was on the Little Temecula Rancho (2,283 acres) held by Pablo Apis, Chief and Representative of the Temeku / Luiseño Indians, under an 1845 Mexican land grant.

There is some dispute amongst researchers as to whether "Magee's Store" (approximate coordinates N33° 28' 32.88", W117° 5' 40.20") or "Wolf's Store" (N33° 28' 45.48", W117° 5' 52.08") was Butterfield's Temecula Station.

Early research including the Conklings appears to site the Butterfield Station at "Wolf's Store" on the north bank of Temecula Creek in the vicinity of what is now Redhawk Parkway at Wolf Store Road. The Wolf's Store site has been preserved in a small historic park but is somewhat hidden behind the Redhawk Town Center shopping Mall. The coordinates N33° 28' 45.48", W117° 5' 52.08" (GPS decimal N33.4793, W117.0978) are immediately at the park site.

Later research maintains that the Wolf's Store location was established in 1868 by Louis Wolf (well after the Butterfield ceased operation in 1861.)

According to the later researchers, John Magee established a store in 1849 on Pablo Apis' Little Temecula Rancho, at the crossroads of the Southern Emigrant Trail and the San Bernardino-to-San Diego Road. Magee's Store, they maintain, became the primary stop for settlers and '49ers traveling the southern route into California.

The Magee Store location appears to have been on the south bank of Temecula Creek in the vicinity of what is now Redhawk Parkway and Overland Trail (to the south and east of the Wolf's Store location). There are also indications that John Magee and Louis Wolf may have cooperated in this "Magee's Store" location during the Butterfield period. Magee's Store and the Apis Adobe on the south side of the creek are reported to have been the heart of the Luiseño community throughout the Butterfield period (1858-1861).

Both of these stores were located on property owned by Pablo Apis and his family. At the present day, Louis Wolf's Store still stands (the oldest building in Temecula), but the Magee Store and Apis Adobe locations have been demolished and the land developed as a suburban residential neighborhood.

In the Fall, 1991, edition of the *Journal of San Diego History* (San Diego Historical Society) is an article entitled "Pablo Apis and Temecula" by Leland E. Bibb. In that article, Bibb maintains: "The earliest reference to John Magee at Temecula is in August, 1858, in Deed Book #1, p. 256, Office of the

Recorder, County of San Diego. His store was on the south side of Temecula Creek some 300 feet easterly of the Indian Village and 900 feet southwesterly of the Apis Adobe."

It is also possible, however, that Magee operated the store by leasehold from Apis (or as the employee of a third party) during the Butterfield period and was given a registered deed and title in 1859.

Historian Anne Miller of Murietta, California, states in correspondence dated October, 2009, that: "In August 1859, María [Apis] leased [the building usually referred to as the Magee Store] to Magee for five years with the provision that he add an addition to the building which he did. That building existed prior to 1859 and in the spring of that year apparently Samuel Prager (a financier from Los Angeles) and his friend Louis Wolf were running a store in the building. Wolf and Magee might have been together in the store for a short time, but Wolf was gone soon after that."

Miller also states with certainty that "The [existing] Wolf Store was not the Butterfield station in Temecula. It was not built until the late 1860s. That [Butterfield] station was on the south side of the creek, not the north."

Brigandi concurs with Miller regarding the Magee's Store location, noting that "I don't believe there is any question among 'scholars' that in the 1850s the Indian village at Temecula was located across the creek, west of where the Wolf Store still stands. John Magee's store was adjacent to the village ... the confusion over the site of the Butterfield station comes from the fact that it was in two different adobes at different times – first in the Apis Adobe, and then in the Magee Store."

What appears certain is that the Temecula Station was in the vicinity of what is now Redhawk Community Park in the 44700 block of Redhawk Parkway (approximate coordinates N33° 28' 34.06", W117° 5' 58.80").

For the purpose of this report we have used the Redhawk Community Park coordinates as a compromise measure given its public accessibility and proximity to both of the reported Butterfield Station sites, although the preserved Wolf Store location is well worth mention in future interpretive material.

The eventual fate of the Apis family and the Luiseños were intertwined. Despite terms of the Treaty of Guadalupe Hidalgo that the United States would recognize the Spanish and Mexican land grants in California, an adjunct 1852 treaty that would have assured Pablo Apis right to his land under American law was rejected -- with the net result that he and his Indian neighbors lost the right to their property. In 1853, the American land commissioners in the area rejected Apis' appeal of the denial of his title, claiming there was nothing to prove exactly where in the Temecula Valley his Little Temecula Rancho grant was located. During this period, Pablo Apis died at the age of 61. The exact date of his death is uncertain, but it is believed to have been between October 22, 1853, and July 10, 1854.

The Apis family, however, continued to press its claims to the Little Temecula Rancho. Another appeal of Apis' title rejection was heard in 1856 and title was granted to Apis' family.

In 1869, another lawsuit was filed by a number of settlers and ranchers seeking eviction of Apis' remaining family and the Luiseños. This lawsuit proved successful, and the family was evicted in 1875. The Luiseño Indian families were removed to the area of what is now the Pechanga Indian Reservation (several miles to the south)and the Little Temecula Rancho passed into history.

Nothing remains of either the Magee or Apis Adobe. As to the fate of the Apis Adobe, Bibb writes:

> "As late as 1865 it was still a store and, evidently, the social center of the Temecula community when it was the subject of a sketch by artist Edward Vischer. Sometime before 1872 it was apparently abandoned. Louis Wolf, pioneer storekeeper of Temecula, acquired the Apis grant in that year and would not have allowed a store to remain in the Apis Adobe in competition with his on the north side of Temecula Creek. Thereafter, the site was completely abandoned and part of a pasture for over an hundred years.

> As a part of the mitigation plan for one of the many housing developments currently being built in Temecula, the Apis adobe was archaeologically excavated in 1989. The foundations of this historic building were bulldozed into oblivion on March 7, 1990."

Ormsby and Bailey both definitively place Temecula as a Butterfield Station site. Hoover also speaks of Temecula in that regard.

Pittman mentions Temecula as a Butterfield site and notes that it was "... the site of the first inland Southern California post office, established in 1859." Brigandi, however, notes that "The notion that Temecula was Southern California's first 'inland' Post Office is an old canard. It was established in 1859, but was preceded by San Bernardino (1852) and Fort Tejon – both fairly inland points ...".

References:

Bailey, Goddard; *California -- Arrival of the Overland Mail -- Itinerary of the Route*; as reported by newspaper article; New York Times (NY) - October 14, 1858

Bailey, Goddard; *Report to Postmaster General A.V. Brown - Full itinerary as reported by De Bow's Review and Industrial Resources, Statistics etc;* published by De Bow's Review; New Orleans and Washington City; 1858. See specifically *Internal Improvements - 1. Wagon Road to the Pacific*; pp 719-721. Internet accessible at http://books.google.com/books?id=5CYoAAAAYAAJ&pg=PA720&lpg=PA720&dq=Cienega+de+los+Pimas&source=bl&ots=_5lZw_Bq23&sig=T6scCb8cpbY7KwjxpYoNvZpcgvI&hl=en&ei=i6KnS6KNOIr2M5yprIED&sa=X&oi=book_result&ct=result&resnum=2&ved=0CAwQ6AEwAQ#v=onepage&q=Cienega%20de%20los%20Pimas&f=false (accessed March 22, 2010)

Bibb, Leland E.; Pablo Apis and Temecula; Journal of San Diego History; San Diego Historical Society; Fall 1991

Conkling, Roscoe P. and Margaret B.; *The Butterfield Overland Mail, 1857–1869* (3 vols); Glendale, CA: A. H.   Clark Company, 1947

Hoover, Mildred Brooke, Hero Eugene Rensch and Ethel Grace Rensch; *Historic Spots in California*; Stanford University Press; Stanford CA; 1932 (rev 1948)

Ormsby, Waterman L.; *The Butterfield Overland Mail (Only Through Passenger on the First Westbound Stage)*; original publications New York Herald (NY) Sep 26 - Nov 19, 1858; republished by Henry E. Huntington Library and Art Gallery, San Marino CA, 1942 - 1998

Pittman, Ruth; *Roadside History of California*; Mountain Press Publishing; Missoula MT; 1995

Temecula, California to Laguna Grande
Prepared by Kirby Sanders

April 25, 2011

Temecula CA (Redhawk Community Park) • Riverside County (N33° 28' 34.06", W117° 5' 58.80")

TO Laguna Grande - Lake Elsinore • Riverside County (N33 39' 47.88", W117 22' 53.32")

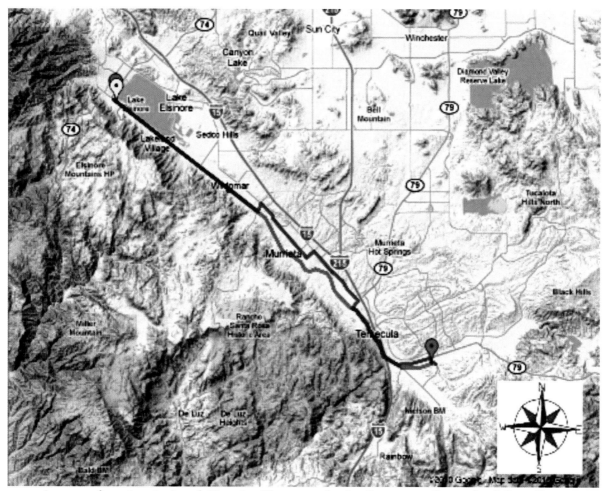

Approximate Actual Route Temecula to Laguna Grande 22 miles.

(1858 Bailey itinerary says 21 miles)

Secondary Landmarks:

Machado Adobe (coordinates N33° 39' 34.82", W117° 22' 50.34"

Notes:

Once again, local research is the foundation for the route approximation through this segment and additional field study would be advised.

Given the facts of topography, however, it does appear that the Butterfield Route through this area followed a northwestward course along the wide valley skirting the Elsinore Mountains -- passing through the modern communities of Temecula, Murrieta and Wildomar into the modern community of Lake Elsinore.

Originally the site of a natural lake fed by 300 natural sulfur springs in the vicinity as well as local rainfall, the original Laguna Grande was eventually expanded to become what would be called Lake Elsinore. The early Luiseño Indian inhabitants of the area believed Laguna Grande and nearby mineral springs to have curative powers. During the Butterfield period, the Laguna Grande / Lake Elsinore site was near the original residence of Augustin Machado and family.

Depending on rainfall, the lake was often dry prior to the 1960s, but beginning in 1964 it received a steady supply of Colorado River water -- and in 1980 flooded the nearby homes and businesses. Thereafter, efforts were made to maintain the lake level as a safe freshwater reservoir. Given that there is no river or other natural outflow from Lake Elsinore, overflow is now diverted into Temescal Canyon.

According to the Lake Elsinore Valley Chamber of Commerce:

> " ... [the] first inhabitants called the lake 'Entengvo Wumoma,' which meant 'Hot Springs by the Little Sea.'
>
> Joining the Native American ... inhabitants, the Spanish missionaries and soldiers, Spanish ranchers and American trappers came to the valley, all stopping to camp and replenish their supplies. They too found the lake, with its hot mineral springs, clear, fresh water and abundance of game to be a pleasant break from the surrounding mountains. The Spanish padres renamed the lake 'Laguna Grande.'
>
> Lake Elsinore was incorporated as a city in 1888 (even before Riverside County's creation in 1893) but was inhabited well

before then. In the early 18th century, when the lake was natural, it provided a spot for Spanish ranchers and American trappers to replenish their supplies [as well]. It was named Elsinore after the Danish city in Shakespeare's 'Hamlet', which is now its sister city.

In the early days of the American occupation of California, Elsinore gained national importance as a campsite for travelers over the Southern Butterfield Stage route, a stagecoach route connecting Saint Louis and San Francisco. Kit Carson and other scouts camped among the cottonwoods on the shores of the lake. The largest army of Civil War volunteers to leave California also set up camp on the lake's shores."

The short-lived Civil War era camp was referred to as "Camp Laguna Grande" and lay along what had come to be called the "Colorado Road" toward Los Angeles – which route appears to have tracked the early de Anza route of 1775-1776.

In 1844, Julian Manriquez was granted the lake and 20,000 acres of surrounding valley. Manriquez subsequently sold the grant to Abel Stearns in 1851. In 1858 Augustin Machado purchased the holding from Stearns and built a home on the south side of the lake. Don Augustin Machado operated a cattle and sheep ranch on the land. He used the uplands to graze his stock during wet years when the lake was high and moved them to the marshes and wetlands when the lake was low. He also operated the Butterfield stage station at his home.

In 1873 Machado's family sold all but 500 acres of their ranch to C.A. Sumner, an English settler. Don Augustin's son, Juan, retained the home and 500 acres.

According to Hoover's 1932 *Historic Spots In California:* "One of the old Machado adobes, possibly the one used as the Butterfield Station, was at 32912 Macy Street near Grand Avenue on the southwest side of Lake Elsinore. It and a small adobe outbuilding have been razed, but the site is marked by three distinctive palm trees. Two rooms of another Machado adobe have been incorporated into the house at 15410 Grand Avenue."

The 1948 revision of Hoover's *Historic Spots in California* (page 34) is less specific than the earlier report, noting that the Machado Butterfield Station "... still stands on Grand Avenue on what is now the Rippey Ranch".

The Macy Street property is located at coordinates N33° 39' 34.82", W117° 22' 50.34".

Anne Miller's research (correspondence as of October, 2009) and Butterfield site mapping prepared by the GIS department of the City of Lake Elsinore both point to the property at the 15410 Grand Avenue address as the proper location of the original Butterfield station (approximate coordinates N33° 39' 47.88", W117° 22' 53.32").

The Macy Street location and the Grand Avenue location are less than 0.5 mile apart. Both are now private homes and should be respected as such.

It is likely that additional information regarding this area might be obtained from the Lake Elsinore Historical Society - they operate a museum and research library in the City of Lake Elsinore's Cultural Center at 183 North Main Street. That facility is open on Wednesdays from 11:00am to 3:00pm.

Ormsby and Bailey both specify Laguna Grande. Pittman identifies it as a Butterfield location as well.

References:

Bailey, Goddard; *California -- Arrival of the Overland Mail -- Itinerary of the Route*; as reported by newspaper article; New York Times (NY) - October 14, 1858

Bailey, Goddard; *Report to Postmaster General A.V. Brown - Full itinerary as reported by De Bow's Review and Industrial Resources, Statistics etc;* published by De Bow's Review; New Orleans and Washington City; 1858. See specifically *Internal Improvements - 1. Wagon Road to the Pacific;* pp 719-721. Internet accessible at http://books.google.com/books?id=5CYoAAAAYAAJ&pg=PA720&lpg=PA720&dq=Cienega+de+los+Pimas&source=bl&ots=_5lZw_Bq23&sig=T6scCb8cpbY7K wjxpYoNvZpcgvI&hl=en&ei=i6KnS6KNOIr2M5yprIED&sa=X&oi=book_result&ct=result&resnum=2&ved=0CAwQ6AEwAQ#v=onepage&q=Cienega%20de%20los%20Pimas&f=false (accessed March 22, 2010)

Conkling, Roscoe P. and Margaret B.; *The Butterfield Overland Mail, 1857–1869* (3 vols); Glendale, CA: A. H. Clark Company, 1947.

Hoover, Mildred Brooke, Hero Eugene Rensch and Ethel Grace Rensch; *Historic Spots in California*; Stanford University Press; Stanford CA; 1932 (rev 1948)

79

Lake Elsinore Valley Chamber of Commerce; *History of Lake Elsinore*; Internet publication accessible at http://www.lakeelsinorechamber.com/city_history.htm

Ormsby, Waterman L.; *The Butterfield Overland Mail (Only Through Passenger on the First Westbound Stage)*; original publications New York Herald (NY) Sep 26 - Nov 19, 1858; republished by Henry E. Huntington Library and Art Gallery, San Marino CA, 1942 - 1998

Pittman, Ruth; *Roadside History of California*; Mountain Press Publishing; Missoula MT; 1995

**Vicinity of Laguna Grande Station - Machado St.
at Grand Ave., Lake Elsinore CA.
Photo by Fred Yeck (2006).**

Laguna Grande to Rancho Temescal
April 26, 2011

Laguna Grande - Lake Elsinore • Riverside County (N33° 39'47.88", W117° 22' 53.32")

TO Rancho Temescal - 20730 Temescal Canyon Road, Corona • Riverside County (N33° 48' 42.09", W117° 30' 18.49")

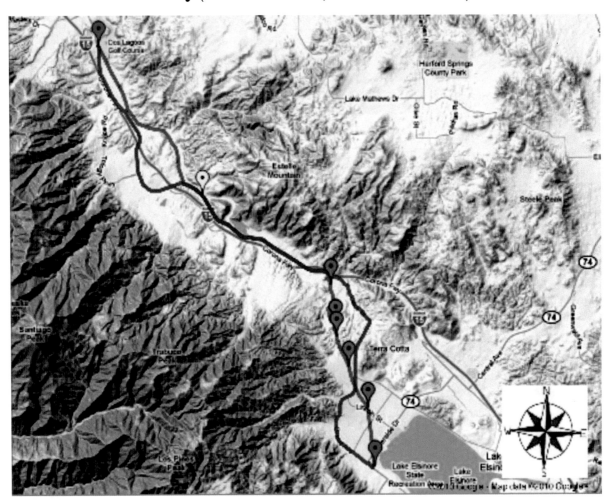

Approximate Actual Route Laguna Grande to Temescal 14 miles.

(1858 Bailey itinerary says 10 miles)

Secondary Landmarks:

Terra Cotta Street northeast of Lincoln Street (Lake Elsinore) - coordinates N33° 41' 1.68", W117° 23' 4.56"

Mountain Street near Palm View Street (Lake Elsinore) - coordinates N33° 41' 54.24", W117° 23' 35.52"

Near the northeast dead-end of Rice Canyon Road (Lake Elsinore) - coordinates N33° 42' 31.68", W117° 23' 54.96"

Private land slightly northeast of the Rice Canyon Road landmark (Lake Elsinore) - coordinates N33° 42' 47.52", W117° 23' 55.68"

"Los Angeles Pressed Brick Company" private land (Alberhill) - approximate coordinates N33° 43' 38.63", W117° 24' 02.97"

Old Temescal Road Historical Marker - Temescal Canyon Road near El Hermano Road - approximate coordinates N33° 45' 31.44", W117° 27' 31.51"

Notes:

The original route from Laguna Grande northward can readily be identified. Anne Miller's research (correspondence dated October, 2009) and the map prepared by the city of Lake Elsinore indicate several points at which traces of the Butterfield Route have been identified and marked as it approached the Temescal Canyon Road. Those markers are located at:

• Terra Cotta Street northeast of Lincoln Street (Lake Elsinore) - coordinates N33° 41' 1.68", W117° 23' 4.56"

• Mountain Street near Palm View Street (Lake Elsinore) - coordinates N33° 41' 54.24", W117° 23' 35.52"

• Near the northeast dead-end of Rice Canyon Road (Lake Elsinore) - coordinates N33° 42' 31.68", W117° 23' 54.96"

• Private land slightly northeast of the Rice Canyon Road mark (Lake Elsinore) - coordinates N33° 42' 47.52", W117° 23' 55.68"

Hoover, Rensch and Rensch (1932) indicate that the route northwestward from Laguna Grande passed through the "Los Angeles Pressed Brick Company" clay quarries and manufacturing plant area on the way to Temescal Canyon Road. Industrial records for the area indicate that the Los Angeles Pressed Brick Company manufacturing plant was located in Alberhill beginning in 1916. Although this property is no longer operated by the Los

Angeles Pressed Brick Company, the location is still a brick manufacturing plant operated by Pacific Clay Products Company -- which bought the Los Angeles Pressed Brick plant in 1963. Approximate coordinates for that site are N33° 43' 38.63", W117° 24' 02.97".

From the northern edge of the "Pacific Clay / Los Angeles Pressed Brick" property, the Butterfield Route essentially tracks what is now Temescal Canyon Road.

There is an intermediate California Historic Site Marker of interest along the way to Rancho Temescal (approximate coordinates N33° 45' 31.44", W117° 27' 31.51"). This marker (#638 Old Temescal Road) helps to mark the route rather than pointing out a specific Butterfield station. The marker reads "This route was used by Luiseño and Gabrieleno Indians, whose villages were nearby. Leandro Serrano established a home here in 1820. [American fur trader David E.] Jackson and [trapper J.J.] Warner traveled the road in 1831, and Frémont in 1848. It was the southern emigrant road for gold seekers from 1849 to 1851, the Overland Mail route from 1858 to 1861, and a military road between Los Angeles and San Diego from 1861 to 1865."

From this marker onward into Temescal, additional route research is advised. The modern Rancho Temescal Road takes a wide loop to the west whereas the canyon itself makes a slight loop toward the east. It is highly likely that the Butterfield Route would have taken the more straightforward course through the valley rather than the modern road route.

The actual Rancho Temescal station site is located to the west of the Dos Lagos Golf Course. Hoover's *Historic Spots* notes that "Horses were changed here in the stables behind the station and, for a time, mail was delivered in the front room of the inn. A very old pepper tree formerly shaded the place, but this has disappeared." Hoover does not cite a source for this information.

As to the California Historic Site marker listed for this location in the state inventory, there is good news and bad news. The good news is that we have the text of that marker from the inventory (#188 Butterfield Stage Station) "Site of Butterfield Stage Station where mail was delivered and horses changed. The first stage carrying overland mail left Tipton, Missouri on September 15, 1858 and, passing through Temescal, arrived in Los Angeles October 7, 1858."

Information from the Dos Lagos Golf Course notes, "The Temescal Stage Stop was located at the northern end of the one mile stretch near the cluster of oak trees that are being preserved as part of the Dos Lagos land plan, in what once was a small citrus orchard. The Temescal Stage Stop provided rest and refreshments to weary travelers, located between Laguna Grande (Lake Elsinore) to the south and San Jose Chino Ranch to the north. Located just east of Temescal Canyon Road, the Temescal Stop is State Historic Landmark #188."

The bad news, as reported by the Dos Lagos development company, is that "An historical landmark plaque was placed at the stage stop site in 1934. The marker, however, was subsequently stolen" -- which leaves the precise location of this station unidentified.

It is possible, however, that additional field research and closer consultation with Dos Lagos Development and local historical organizations might pinpoint a reasonably definitive location.

Bailey and Ormsby both specifically mention Temescal.

Coordinates for this location are N33° 48' 42.09", W117° 30' 18.49"

References:

Bailey, Goddard; *California -- Arrival of the Overland Mail -- Itinerary of the Route*; as reported by newspaper article; New York Times (NY) - October 14, 1858

Bailey, Goddard; *Report to Postmaster General A.V. Brown - Full itinerary as reported by De Bow's Review and Industrial Resources, Statistics etc;* published by De Bow's Review; New Orleans and Washington City; 1858. See specifically *Internal Improvements - 1. Wagon Road to the Pacific*; pp 719-721. Internet accessible at http://books.google.com/books?id=5CYoAAAAYAAJ&pg=PA720&lpg=PA720&dq=Cienega+de+los+Pimas&source=bl&ots=_5lZw_Bq23&sig=T6scCb8cpbY7K wjxpYoNvZpcgvI&hl=en&ei=i6KnS6KNOIr2M5yprIED&sa=X&oi=book_result&ct=result&resnum=2&ved=__0CAwQ6AEwAQ#v=onepage&q=Cienega%20de%20los%20Pimas&f=false (accessed March 22, 2010)

California State Parks - Office of Historic Preservation; California Historical Landmarks; Internet database - http://www.parks.ca.gov/default.asp?page_id=21387 (accessed April 4, 2010)

Conkling, Roscoe P. and Margaret B.; *The Butterfield Overland Mail, 1857–1869* (3 vols); Glendale, CA: A. H. Clark Company, 1947

Dos Lagos Golf Course; *Course History;* Internet publication accessible at http://www.doslagosgolf.com/page/271-11676.htm (accessed 31 May, 2010)

Hoover, Mildred Brooke, Hero Eugene Rensch and Ethel Grace Rensch; *Historic Spots in California*; Stanford University Press; Stanford CA; 1932 (rev 1948)

Ormsby, Waterman L.; *The Butterfield Overland Mail (Only Through Passenger on the First Westbound Stage)*; original publications New York Herald (NY) Sep 26 - Nov 19, 1858; republished by Henry E. Huntington Library and Art Gallery, San Marino CA, 1942 - 1998.

Temescal Station historical marker at Dos Lagos Shopping Center(N33.81628, W117.50847). Photo by Fred Yeck (2006).

Temescal to Ranch Chino
December 30, 2010

Rancho Temescal - 20730 Temescal Canyon Road, Corona• Riverside County (N33° 48' 42.09", W117° 30' 18.49")

TO Rancho Chino - 4040 Eucalyptus Avenue; Chino, CA • San Bernardino County (N33° 59' 23.28", W117° 43' 03.42")

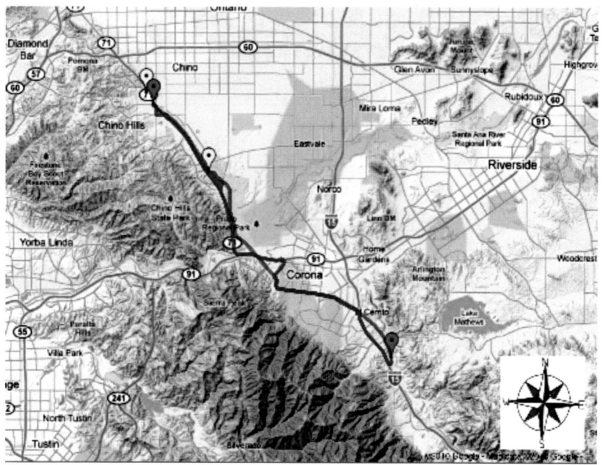

Approximate Actual Route Temescal to Rancho Chino 19 miles.

(1858 Bailey itinerary says 20 miles)

Secondary Landmarks:

Rancho Rincon / Yorba-Slaughter Adobe - 17127 Pomona Rincon Road, Chino - approximate coordinates N33° 56' 30.57", W117° 40' 05.68"

Boys Republic High School - 3493 Grand Avenue, Chino Hills - coordinates N33° 59' 51.23", W117° 43' 27.62"

Notes:

The Butterfield Route from Temescal to Rancho Chino can be determined with some degree of accuracy. In correspondence dated November 7, 2010, local historian Phil Brigandi states that the Butterfield Route out of Temescal followed Temescal Canyon Road.

Slightly north of Temescal, it appears the Butterfield Route trimmed westward along the foothills, roughly tracking through Corona along what is now Ontario Avenue to about Paseo Grande -- at which point the original Butterfield Route appears to have gone "off-road" in modern terms.

The route appears to have tracked briefly along what is now Palisades Drive and then into what is now the Butterfield Stage Trail Park in Corona. Of this vicinity specifically, Brigandi noted "It would appear (but should be confirmed) that the Butterfield crossed the Santa Ana river ... near where the Prado Dam is today."

The route then appears to track into the historic Pomona Rincon Road slightly east of the modern Highway 71. Says Brigandi, "the natural route would certainly seem to be along Chino Creek, which both the Pomona Rincon Road and the 71 Corona Expressway parallel."

California Historical Site Marker #191 marks an intermediate point of interest on the next leg from Rancho Temescal to Rancho Chino. The intermediate site is Rancho Rincon, also known as the Yorba-Slaughter Adobe (17127 Pomona - Rincon Road, approximate coordinates N33° 56' 30.57", W117° 40' 05.68").

While neither Ormsby nor Bailey mentions the Yorba-Slaughter / Rancho Rincon site, Hoover, Rensch and Rensch among others mention the location as having been an occasional Butterfield station (possibly a "flag stop").

The Yorba-Slaughter adobe is a branch museum of the San Bernardino County Museum and is also listed on the National Register of Historic Places (1975 - #75000460).

The historical marker at the site notes "This example of early California architecture was built in 1850-53 by Raimundo Yorba. Purchased in 1868 by Fenton Mercer Slaughter, it was preserved as a memorial to him by his daughter, Julia Slaughter Fuqua."

According to information from the San Bernardino County Museum, "The Yorba family was among the most influential in the early history of the Prado Basin. José Antonio Yorba was granted the Rancho Santiago de Santa Ana, 60,000 acres between present-day San Diego and Santa Ana, in 1801. His son, Bernardo Yorba, added to the family holdings with the purchase of 18,000 acres in the Rincon area from Juan Bandini. Bernardo's son, Raymundo (also spelled Raimundo) built the first house at the Yorba-Slaughter Adobe site in 1851. The structure burned and was replaced by the present structure in 1852-53. The adobe, built by Indian laborers from a rancheria east of the property, was known as "Buena Vista." The road at the foot of the hill was a regularly used part of the Fort Yuma to Los Angeles Road, and the Yorba Adobe was an optional stage stop for the Butterfield Overland Mail from 1858 to the start of the Civil War. The rancho was prosperous, and Raymundo Yorba was the most affluent of the land owners in the Prado Basin."

As to the station itself, the museum information continues:

> "The adobe residence was originally one story with a sleeping loft: the four rooms on the main floor and 3 in the loft were arranged side-by-side. Nearly every room had an exterior door. Wide porches were built on all four sides; porches on the east and south sides were later enclosed.
>
> Next door, the ornamental concrete block house was built between 1906 and 1909. It, too, had porches that were later framed to create more rooms. It was to become the principal residence at Buena Vista; the adobe was apparently unoccupied between 1916 and 1929 and was for a time used to grow mushrooms.
>
> Restoration of the adobe was started in 1928 by Julia Slaughter Fuqua, the third child of Fenton and Dolores Slaughter. The adobe was designated California State Historical Landmark #191 in 1934, and the property was purchased by the County of San

Bernardino in 1971. Major restoration and seismic retrofitting of the adobe was completed in September, 2000."

The Yorba-Slaughter Adobe is listed on the National Register of Historic Places (1975 - #75000460).

Northwest of the adobe, the Butterfield Route continues to track Chino Creek in the vicinity of modern Highway 71 to Rancho Chino / Williams Ranch Station.

The Rancho Chino Station was located on land acquired as the Rancho Santa Ana del Chino by Antonio Maria Lugo. In 1841, Lugo deeded a half-interest in the property to his son-in-law, Col. Isaac Williams. By 1851, Lugo had deeded full ownership of the property to his son-in-law.

Williams built an adobe mansion and ranching compound at the site which included livestock barns, shearing sheds, huts and dormitories for laborers and caballeros, and a grist mill. He planted orchards and vineyards as well as other food crops and maintained cattle, horses and sheep on his lands. Williams also carried out a bustling trade in hides and tallow.

During 1846, the Rancho was the site of an important skirmish between Californians and Americans during the Mexican War.

Upon Williams' death in 1856, his wife, Mercedes, remarried and moved from the property, leaving their daughter Francesca and her husband Robert Carlisle in charge of Rancho Chino.

In 1858 the Carlisles contracted with John Butterfield to operate the stage station at this site.

Unfortunately, nothing of the original buildings remain at Rancho Chino. There is a California Historical marker in the area (#942 — The Rancho Chino Adobe of Isaac Williams). That marker is located in front of the Chino Hills Fire Station Nr. 2 at 4040 Eucalyptus Avenue (coordinates N33° 59' 23.28", W117° 43' 03.42"), which is the location specified in this report.

The marker states "Near this site, Isaac Williams in 1841 built a large adobe home, located on the 22,000-acre Rancho Chino which he acquired from his father-in-law Antonio Lugo. The "Battle of Chino" occurred at the adobe on September 26-27, 1846, during which 24 Americans were captured by a group of about 50 Californios. Located on the Southern Immigrant Trail to California, the adobe later became an inn and stage stop famous for its hospitality."

With reference to that marker denoting the station location as having been "***near*** this site", some local residents indicate the specific site of the adobe station to have been on what is now private property in the vicinity of the Boys Republic facility at 3493 Grand Avenue, Chino Hills CA (coordinates N33° 59' 51.23", W117° 43' 27.62"). That location is approximately one-half mile north and slightly west of the Fire Station marker.

Ormsby and Bailey both specifically mention Rancho Chino. Hoover, Rensch and Rensch discuss both Rancho Rincon and Rancho Chino

References:

Bailey, Goddard; *California -- Arrival of the Overland Mail -- Itinerary of the Route*; as reported by newspaper article; New York Times (NY) - October 14, 1858

Bailey, Goddard; *Report to Postmaster General A.V. Brown - Full itinerary as reported by De Bow's Review and Industrial Resources, Statistics etc*; published by De Bow's Review; New Orleans and Washington City; 1858. See specifically *Internal Improvements - 1. Wagon Road to the Pacific*; pp 719-721. Internet accessible at http://books.google.com/books?id=5CYoAAAAYAAJ&pg=PA720&lpg=PA720& dq=Cienega+de+los+Pimas&source=bl&ots=_5lZw_Bq23&sig=T6scCb8cpbY7K wjxpYoNvZpcgvI&hl=en&ei=i6KnS6KNOIr2M5yprIED&sa=X&oi=book_result& ct=result&resnum=2&ved=_0CAwQ6AEwAQ#v=onepage&q=Cienega%20de% 20los%20Pimas&f=false (accessed March 22, 2010)

Conkling, Roscoe P. and Margaret B.; *The Butterfield Overland Mail, 1857–1869* (3 vols); Glendale, CA: A. H. Clark Company, 1947

California State Parks - Office of Historic Preservation; California Historical Landmarks; Internet database - http://www.parks.ca.gov/default.asp?page_id=21387 (accessed April 4, 2010)

Hoover, Mildred Brooke, Hero Eugene Rensch and Ethel Grace Rensch; *Historic Spots in California*; Stanford University Press; Stanford CA; 1932 (rev 1948)

National Register of Historic Places; *National Register Locations by State*; Internet publication; accessible at

http://www.nationalregisterofhistoricplaces.com/state.html (accessed May 3, 2010)

Ormsby, Waterman L.; *The Butterfield Overland Mail (Only Through Passenger on the First Westbound Stage)*; original publications New York Herald (NY) Sep 26 - Nov 19, 1858; republished by Henry E. Huntington Library and Art Gallery, San Marino CA, 1942 - 1998

San Bernardino County Museum; *The Yorba and Slaughter Families Adobe*; Internet publication accessible at http://www.co.san-bernardino.ca.us/museum/branches/yorba.htm (accessed May 31, 2010)

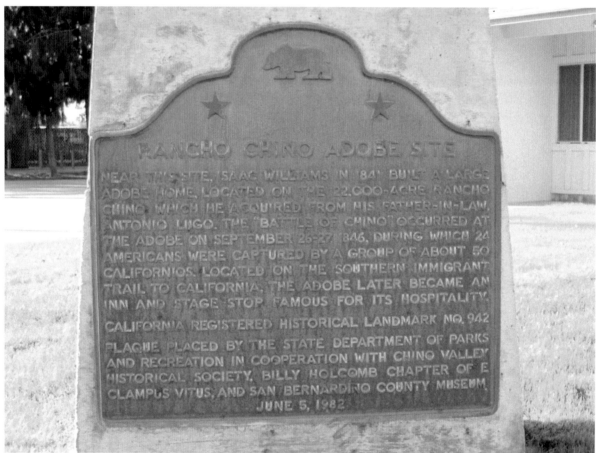

**Rancho Chino historical marker
(N33.9900, W117.7177).
Photo by Fred Yeck (2008).**

Rancho Chino to San Jose, California
January 15, 2012

Rancho Chino - 4040 Eucalyptus Avenue; Chino, CA • San Bernardino County (N33° 59' 23.28", W117° 43' 03.42")

TO Rancho San Jose de Arriba; La Puente Road at Old Post Road; Walnut CA • Los Angeles County (N34° 1' 22.80", W117° 51' 28.80")

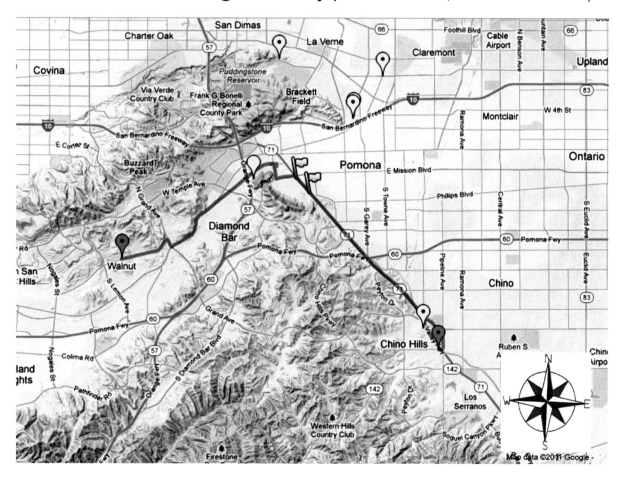

Approximate Actual Route, Rancho Chino to Rancho San Jose

de Arriba 12 miles (1858 Bailey itinerary says 12 miles)

Secondary Landmarks:

Boys Republic High School - 3493 Grand Avenue, Chino Hills - N33° 59' 51.23", W117° 43' 27.62"

Butterfield Road segments, Pomona CA – both sides of Chino Valley Freeway between W Phillips Boulevard and Vejar / Fleming Streets

Spadra CA (landmark) - N34° 3' 7.20", W117° 48' 0.00"

Palomares "Casa Primera" (landmark) - 1569 North Park Avenue, Pomona CA – N34° 04' 30.77", W117° 45' 18.28"

Casa Madera / Adobe de Palomares / Palomares Park (landmark) - 491 East Arrow Highway - N34° 5' 23.86", W117° 44' 33.18"

Casa Alvarado (landmark) - 1469 Old Settlers Lane, Pomona CA – N34° 04' 27.39", W117° 45' 20.41"

Carrion Adobe (landmark) - 919 Puddingstone Drive, Pomona CA – N34° 06' 46.56", W117° 47' 18.91"

Notes:

Local research on the Butterfield Route from Rancho Chino to Rancho San Jose indicates that the route ran parallel to Chino Creek along the west bank on a northerly course toward what is now Pomona CA. That route roughly tracks the modern course of the Chino Valley Freeway. On the western edge of modern Pomona, the route then tracks westward via the community of Spadra to what is now the town of Walnut. Also notable in this regard is the fact that there two segments of modern road in southwestern Pomona named "Butterfield Road." Those segments track on both sides of the Chino Valley Freeway between W Phillips Boulevard and Vejar Street on the east side of the freeway and / Fleming Street on the west side of the freeway.

The next Butterfield stop, often referred to in shorthand as "San Jose", can cause some confusion. During the Butterfield Period there were two properties referred to as "Rancho San Jose" -- operated by two friends in this area. The first of these, Rancho San Jose de Arriba (Upper Rancho San Jose), was the Butterfield station site operated by Don Ygnacio Palomares and family.

The other Rancho San Jose (Rancho San Jose de Abajo) was established by Ricardo Vejar. It was located in to the southwest of the Rancho de Arriba holdings.

While there are indications that the Butterfield Station was at the main Hacienda of the Rancho San Jose de Arriba -- the Adobe de Palomares (491 East Arrow Highway, Pomona CA; coordinates N34° 5' 23.86", W117° 44' 33.18") -- the mileage to that location falls several miles short of Bailey's reported mileage. Additionally, Casa Palomares lies well to the northeast of the Rancho San Jose station according to the Conklings.

According to information from the Pomona Valley historical society, "The one story, L-shaped building containing thirteen rooms was built in the ranch-house style. It features a corridor around the outer perimeter, a shingle shake roof and sailing-cloth ceilings. The Adobe and stagecoach stop was known as the 'House of Hospitality'. The Adobe was abandoned for many years until it was taken over by the City of Pomona in 1930 and restored through community efforts. The restoration was completed in 1940. Most of the rooms are authentically furnished with many items belonging to the original adobe. The site is maintained and opened to the public by the Historical Society of Pomona Valley, Inc."

The Conklings state quite specifically, however, that the Butterfield "pass(ed) through what is now Spadra and along the west bank of San Jose Creek to San Jose Ranch. San Jose Ranch station (was) twelve miles northwest of Chino Ranch" and that "The station at San Jose Ranch, which was a small change station, was located on an old site known as Mission Graneros ... the site which is located one half mile northeast of Walnut."

Butterfield researcher Fred Yeck followed the Conklings' directions to this site in modern terms. During a visit to the area, Yeck placed the Rancho San Jose by on-site GPS reading at coordinates N34.023, W117.858 (N34° 1' 22.80", W117° 51' 28.80"); La Puente Road at Old Post Road. Yeck reported, "The frontage road on either side of CA 71 just south of Mission Boulevard is called Butterfield Road. Measuring ½ mile northeast of Walnut on La Puente Road we found Old Post Road which is the entrance to an area of new homes at N34.023, W117.858."
Yeck reported no ruins or remnants of the original station.

Conklings also noted that the Butterfield station was at "the home of E. R. Foster" during the 1930s. It is possible that a close investigation of land records for this area during that time can more clearly determine the exact location of the site.

While we will speak substantially of the Casa Palomares and vicinity in this report as the hub and "nerve center" of the Rancho San Jose de Arriba, it is quite obvious that the Butterfield Station was located at the Walnut site rather than at the main hacienda in Palomares Park. There are original structures from the Butterfield period at these additional locations, however. Thus, they also serve researchers by giving them an opportunity to visit historic structures from the time.

Rancho San Jose de Arriba was the home of Don Ygnacio Palomares; the ranch was first settled under an 1837 land grant. Like many of the ranchos in the area, the Rancho San Jose properties were sold into private hands after the original Mission San Gabriel was secularized and its landholdings dispersed.

The Palomares family's first home ("Casa Primera") is located at 1569 North Park Avenue in Pomona (coordinates N34° 04' 30.77", W117° 45' 18.28"). It is described in John R. Kielbasa's *Historic Adobes of Los Angeles County* (Dorrance Publishing Co. 1998), "After Palomares received his San Jose grant in 1837, he began construction of his adobe house. He chose a site just south of the hills, which is today, Ganesha Park. This house, credited as being the first structure in the Pomona Valley, became known as 'La Casa Primera', (The First House). It was the first of two adobe homes Don Ygnacio built for his family on Rancho San Jose. It was a single story house that consisted of five rooms arranged in a row. It had a wide, lengthy corridor along the front and wrapped around one of the sides. The roof was supported by slender wooden posts, probably from trees brought down from the Mount San Antonio. On the north side, there was a wood staircase that led to an attic. The house was typical of that era."

La Casa Primera de Rancho San Jose is maintained as an historical site by the Historical Society of Pomona Valley.

According to the Pomona Valley historical society:

The Casa [Primera] was the first home of Don Ygnacio Palomares, who along with Don Ricardo Vejar, was one of the original grantees of the Rancho San Jose. The Casa was built in 1837 and was the first residential dwelling in the Pomona Valley. The Palomares family lived here for seventeen years before moving to the larger Adobe de Palomares site. In 1867 the Palomares' son Don Francisco occupied the Casa. He discovered the first artesian well and planted orange trees, some of which still survive on the property. The old stone-lined water ditch is still visible. Don Francisco was known for his involvement in several civic activities, including the school board. After a succession of owners, in 1973 the City of Pomona purchased the Casa. In 1986 the adobe was restored by the Society with the help of the California Historic Preservation Grant, plus financial assistance from the City. The adobe won the 1991 'Design Award' given by the California Preservation Foundation. It is furnished with authentic 19th Century furnishings by the Historical Society of Pomona Valley, Inc. The Casa features sod adobe construction, one and one half stories, gabled roof, and front and side wrap around porch.

Between 1850 and 1854, Don Ygnacio had built a second house on an area he called his 'San Antonio Vineyard', which was along the old San Bernardino Road which cut through his section of the rancho. 'La Casa Madera', as it became known, was a much larger house. It had fifteen rooms to better accommodate his large family. The 'T' shaped house had a cloth ceiling and a hipped roof made of shake. Like La Casa Primera, it was a single story structure and had an exterior corridor, which wrapped around the "T" portion. The original house had a corridor facing the patio as well. The old San Bernardino Road (now Arrow Highway) was the main path to all points east. It was a busy freight route and was well used by immigrants. In 1858, the famous Butterfield Stage Route started to use the old road on the way to San Francisco from Saint Louis, Missouri. La Casa Madera became a popular way station for anyone wishing to take a respite from the long arduous journey. Don Ygnacio and Dona China were always the most amicable hosts.

The "Casa Madera" at this location (coordinates N34° 5' 23.86", W117° 44' 33.18") is also recognized with a California Historical Sites Marker (#372 Adobe de Palomares) which reads "Completed about 1854 and restored in 1939, this was the family home of Don Ygnacio Palomares. Governor Juan B. Alvarado granted Rancho San Jose to Don Ygnacio and Don Ricardo Vejar in 1837."

As to the latter history of the building, Kielbasa writes:

"Adobe de Palomares or 'La Casa Madera' (The Wooden House) was so named because its roof was made of wood. Hand cut wood beams came from the Mormon mill in the San Bernardino Mountains. The Meserve family lived in the house when Dona Concepcion sold the property. They stayed for about ten years. Afterward, the place became a roadside tavern and rest stop. It boasted a huge fireplace in the sala (living room) which travelers would gather to warm themselves on cold winter evenings. Eventually, the adobe was abandoned and left defenseless to vandals, thieves, and the elements. The rains eroded away the exposed adobe walls causing the heavy roof to cave in. By 1934, the old house was reduced to ruins. The city of Pomona had since purchased the adobe and planned to build a reservoir on the site. Various community groups led by the Pomona Valley Historical Society led to a concerted effort to raise money to save the historic vestige. The campaign was a success and the city of Pomona sponsored the restoration.

Work began in 1939 to reconstruct the ailing structure, which by that time all that was left standing was the east and west wings. Tremendous pains went into research to assist with the restoration process in order to replace everything as it originally appeared. Even the gardens and trees were replanted in original locations. Approximately 25,000 adobe bricks were made on the grounds much in the same way as the early days. Many of the original broken bricks were repaired and replaced. On April 4, 1940, the restoration was complete and a grand dedication celebration took place with surviving members of the Palomares families attending in costumes of the period of Don Ygnacio and Dona Concepcion. Porfirio Palomares, one of the grandsons of Don Ygnacio, and his family lived in the north section of the house. The house was open for public display with Porfirio Palomares welcoming all who entered."

The Casa Madera / Ygnacio Palomares Adobe is listed on the National Register of Historic Places (1971 - #71000156).

Located nearby is another historic adobe, Casa Alvarado (1469 Old Settlers Lane – coordinates N34° 04' 27.39", W117° 45' 20.41"). Kielbasa reports that the Casa Alvarado was built in 1840 by Ygnacio Alvarado, a close friend of Don Ygnacio Palomares.

Bailey and Ormsby both mention the Rancho San Jose Station.

References:

Bailey, Goddard; *California -- Arrival of the Overland Mail -- Itinerary of the Route*; as reported by newspaper article; *New York Times* (NY) - October 14, 1858.

Bailey, Goddard; *Report to Postmaster General A.V. Brown - Full itinerary as reported by De Bow's Review and Industrial Resources, Statistics etc;* published by De Bow's Review; New Orleans and Washington City; 1858. See specifically *Internal Improvements - 1. Wagon Road to the Pacific*; pp 719-721. Internet accessible at http://books.google.com/books?id=5CYoAAAAYAAJ&pg=PA720&lpg=PA720&dq=Cienega+de+los+Pimas&source=bl&ots=_5lZw_Bq23&sig=T6scCb8cpbY7KwjxpYoNvZpcgvI&hl=en&ei=i6KnS6KNOIr2M5yprIED&sa=X&oi=book_result&ct=result&resnum=2&ved=_0CAwQ6AEwAQ#v=onepage&q=Cienega%20de%20los%20Pimas&f=false (accessed March 22, 2010).

Conkling, Roscoe P. and Margaret B.; *The Butterfield Overland Mail, 1857–1869* (3 vols.); Glendale, CA: A. H. Clark Company, 1947.

California State Parks - Office of Historic Preservation; California Historical Landmarks; Internet database - http://www.parks.ca.gov/default.asp?page_id=21387 (accessed April 4, 2010).

Kielbasa, John R.; *Historic Adobes of Los Angeles County*; Dorrance Publishing Co; Pittsburgh (July 1998); Internet publication (partial) Things to Do in Los Angeles; http://www.laokay.com/halac/ (accessed March 9, 2010).

National Register of Historic Places; *National Register Locations by State*; Internet publication; accessible at

http://www.nationalregisterofhistoricplaces.com/state.html (accessed May 3, 2010).

Ormsby, Waterman L.; *The Butterfield Overland Mail (Only Through Passenger on the First Westbound Stage)*; original publications *New York Herald* (NY) Sep 26 - Nov 19, 1858; republished by Henry E. Huntington Library and Art Gallery, San Marino CA, 1942 – 1998.

Pomona Valley Historical Society; *Pomona Valley History*; Internet publication accessible at http://www.pomonahistorical.org/throw/default.htm (accessed May 31, 2010).

Yeck, Fred; *The Butterfield Overland Mail*; 2011 – unpublished monograph supplied by the author.

San Jose, California to El Monte, California
April 27, 2011

Rancho San Jose de Arriba- 491 East Arrow Highway; Pomona • Los Angeles County (N34° 5' 23.86", W117° 44' 33.18")

TO El Monte (Willow Grove Inn) - 11333 Valley Boulevard; El   Monte • Los Angeles County (N34° 4' 14.90", W118° 1' 50.14")

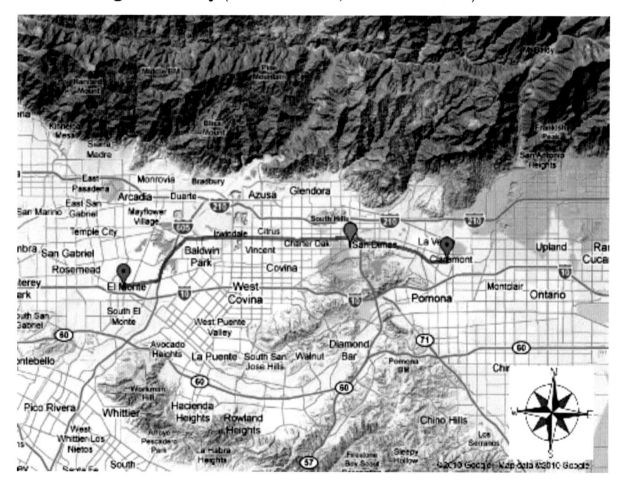

Approximate Actual Route Ranch San Jose de Arriba to El Monte (Willow Grove) 18.4 miles.

(1858 Bailey itinerary says 12 miles)

Secondary Landmarks:

Alternative possibility Rancho San Jose Station - Lone Hill AV and Arrow Highway, San Dimas.

Notes:

• Data update as of April 2013 • Again. Researcher Fred Yeck presents compelling evidence that this route is incorrect and requires further review. Yeck maintains (with solid evidence via the Conklings' data) that the route went from the Rancho Sano Jose station site in Walnut, California along what is now Valley Boulevard to the station in El Monte.

From Rancho San Jose de Arriba to Willow Grove, the Butterfield Route again essentially followed one of the de Anza routes of 1775 - 1776.

In modern terms, the historic road toward Los Angeles from de Anza forward essentially tracked the modern Arrow Highway to the vicinity of Rivergrade Road in Baldwin Park where it dropped southerly along the San Gabriel River to a crossing in the vicinity of what is now Ramona Boulevard. At this point, the Butterfield Route took a southwesterly course to the next station-- the Willow Grove Inn.

Willow Grove on the Butterfield Route can be definitively located at the modern-day location of the El Monte City Hall.

Again, however, this definitive location does not fit Bailey's mileage measurement from Rancho San Jose if that station is assumed to have been at the Palomares Adobe location in Pomona CA. An alternative placement of the Rancho San Jose near Lone Hill AV and Arrow Highway in San Dimas, however, brings the comparative mileage to within one mile of Bailey's report.

An article titled *A Brief History of El Monte* by Jack Barton of the El Monte Historical Museum reports that the Willow Grove Inn was established by members of the Thompson Family Party, emigrants from Iowa who arrived in the area in 1851. Reportedly, the family had come to California in search of gold. Wearied by the travails of crossing the Sonora and Colorado deserts, however, they opted for farming when they arrived at the oasis of "The Island."

As an adjunct to the farm, they also opened their home and land to other emigrants for lodging and camping. Specifically, Barton writes that "The Willow Grove Inn, [was] established, owned and operated by the self-same first pioneer Thompson Family, and [was] a regular way station on the Butterfield Stage route between Riverside and Los Angeles."

Hoover's *Historic Spots In California* cites the Willow Grove Inn as being "on what is now the site of the Valley Dairy and Ice Cream Factory," which was probably quite helpful when that book was published in 1932. The Valley Dairy, however is now defunct.

According to information from a 2009 telephone interview with staff at the El Monte Historical Museum, the old dairy site is now the location of the El Monte City Hall at 11333 Valley Boulevard.

Nothing remains of the old Willow Grove Inn Butterfield Station. Bailey and Ormsby specifically mention the El Monte Station. Ormsby notes that "The Post Office is a wooden building, with a neat piazza and shingled roof, which looked quite refreshing after over a thousand miles' travel without seeing a house having the appearance of civilization."

References:

Bailey, Goddard; *California -- Arrival of the Overland Mail -- Itinerary of the Route*; as reported by newspaper article; New York Times (NY) - October 14, 1858

Bailey, Goddard; *Report to Postmaster General A.V. Brown - Full itinerary as reported by De Bow's Review and Industrial Resources, Statistics etc*; published by De Bow's Review; New Orleans and Washington City; 1858. See specifically *Internal Improvements - 1. Wagon Road to the Pacific*; pp 719-721. Internet accessible at http://books.google.com/books?id=5CYoAAAAYAAJ&pg=PA720&lpg=PA720& dq=Cienega+de+los+Pimas&source=bl&ots=_5lZw_Bq23&sig=T6scCb8cpbY7K wjxpYoNvZpcgvI&hl=en&ei=i6KnS6KNOIr2M5yprIED&sa=X&oi=book_result& ct=result&resnum=2&ved=__0CAwQ6AEwAQ#v=onepage&q=Cienega%20de% 20los%20Pimas&f=false (accessed March 22, 2010)

Barton Jack; *A Brief History of El Monte*; El Monte Historical Museum; Internet publication accessible at http://home.earthlink.net/~jackbarton/ElMonteHistory.htm (accessed May 31, 2010)

Conkling, Roscoe P. and Margaret B.; *The Butterfield Overland Mail, 1857–1869* (3 vols); Glendale, CA: A. H. Clark Company, 1947

Hoover, Mildred Brooke; Hero Eugene Rensch and Ethel Grace Rensch; *Historic Spots in California*; Stanford University Press; Stanford CA; 1932 (rev 1948)

National Park Service; *Juan Bautista de Anza National Historic Trail Guide Los Angeles County CA)*; Internet publication available at http://www.solideas.com/DeAnza/TrailGuide/Los_Angeles/index.html (accessed July 28, 2010)

Ormsby, Waterman L.; *The Butterfield Overland Mail (Only Through Passenger on the First Westbound Stage)*; original publications New York Herald (NY) Sep 26 - Nov 19, 1858; republished by Henry E. Huntington Library and Art Gallery, San Marino CA, 1942 - 1998

Pomona Valley Historical Society; *Pomona Valley History*; Internet publication accessible at http://www.pomonahistorical.org/throw/default.htm (accessed May 31, 2010)

Old Photo of Willow Grove Station - circa 1870 (N34.070, W118.030). Courtesy Fred Yeck (2011).

El Monte, California to Los Angeles
April 27, 2011

El Monte (Willow Grove Inn) - 11333 Valley Boulevard; El Monte • Los Angeles County (N34° 4' 14.90", W118° 1' 50.14")

TO Mirror Building / 1860 Butterfield Station - 145 S Spring Street; Los Angeles • Los Angeles County (N34° 3' 8.53", W118° 14' 42.00")

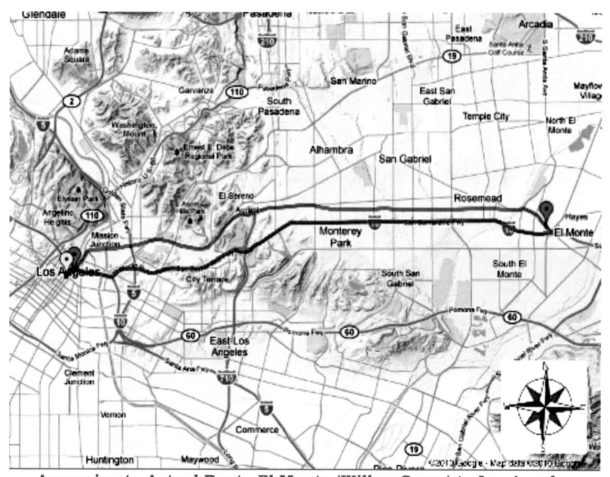

Approximate Actual Route El Monte (Willow Grove) to Los Angeles

14 miles.

(1858 Bailey itinerary says 13 miles)

Secondary Landmarks:

Bella Union Hotel (first Butterfield station) - 314 N Main Street. Los Angeles - approximate coordinates N34° 3' 15.11", W118° 14' 29.59"

Notes:

From El Monte / Willow Grove, the Butterfield continued westward into the heart of Los Angeles. From modern El Monte to about Rosemead, the Butterfield followed the de Anza Route 1775 - 1776. At about Rosemead, however, the de Anza route trimmed to the northwest while the Butterfield continued on a due westerly course.

In modern terms, that route essentially tracks present day Valley Boulevard to the vicinity of Mission Junction where it crossed the Los Angeles River into downtown Los Angeles.

When the Overland Mail runs began in 1858, Butterfield rented space at the Bella Union Hotel in the central plaza until company-owned facilities could be completed. By 1860, the station moved to a site at what later became the Mirror Building, early home of one of the precursor publications to the Times-Mirror newspaper.

The site of the Bella Union Hotel is presently buried beneath the Los Angeles Mall at 314 N Main Street (near coordinates N34° 3' 15.11", W118° 14' 29.59").

Originally, the Bella Union was a single-story adobe constructed in 1835 as the home of Isaac Williams. Williams was a merchant from New England who had moved to Los Angeles in 1832. The building was purchased in 1845 by territorial governor Pio Pico.

After American forces conquered the city in 1847, the building was used by Lt. Archibald Gillespie and housed American occupation troops. It operated briefly as a saloon after the occupation forces relinquished control of the building. By early 1850, the Bella Union Hotel (the first hotel in Los Angeles) had opened in the one story building. A second story was added to the Bella Union in 1851 and a third was added after the Butterfield period in 1869.

In 1858, the Overland Mail Company rented space at the Bella Union for a station. The Wells, Fargo Company also had their office here. A local stageline owned by Phineas Banning operated coach service to Wilmington and San Bernardino from the Bella Union as well. The first westbound

Butterfield Overland Mail stage arrived at the Bella Union on October 7, 1858, only 21 days after leaving Saint Louis.

There is a California Historical Sites Marker at this location (#656 Bella Union Hotel) which states "Near this spot stood the Bella Union Hotel, long a social and political center. Here, on October 7, 1858, the first Butterfield Overland Mail stage from the east arrived 21 days after leaving Saint Louis. Warren Hall was the driver, and Waterman Ormsby, a reporter, the only through passenger."

In 1860, the Butterfield station moved to their own digs about a half-mile southwest of the Bella Union at 145 S Spring Street (coordinates (N34° 3' 8.53", W118° 14' 42.00"). Nothing remains of the old Butterfield Station.

A California Historical Sites marker (#744 The Mirror Building / Site of Butterfield Stage Station) at this second location says "The Butterfield Overland Mail Company took an option on this piece of property in August 1858 and acquired it on December 7, 1859. A large brick building containing offices and living quarters, with shops and stables in the rear, was completed in 1860. With the exception of the station at El Paso, Texas, this was the largest and best equipped station on the entire route."

Bailey and Ormsby specifically mention the Los Angeles Station. Hoover writes in depth about Los Angeles and its growth as a commercial center during the Butterfield period.

References:

Bailey, Goddard; *California -- Arrival of the Overland Mail -- Itinerary of the Route*; as reported by newspaper article; New York Times (NY) - October 14, 1858

Bailey, Goddard; *Report to Postmaster General A.V. Brown - Full itinerary as reported by De Bow's Review and Industrial Resources, Statistics etc;* published by De Bow's Review; New Orleans and Washington City; 1858. See specifically *Internal Improvements - 1. Wagon Road to the Pacific*; pp 719-721. Internet accessible at http://books.google.com/books?id=5CYoAAAAYAAJ&pg=PA720&lpg=PA720&dq=Cienega+de+los+Pimas&source=bl&ots=_5lZw_Bq23&sig=T6scCb8cpbY7KwjxpYoNvZpcgvI&hl=en&ei=i6KnS6KNOIr2M5yprIED&sa=X&oi=book_result&ct=result&resnum=2&ved=_0CAwQ6AEwAQ#v=onepage&q=Cienega%20de%20los%20Pimas&f=false (accessed March 22, 2010)

California State Parks - Office of Historic Preservation; California Historical Landmarks; Internet database - http://www.parks.ca.gov/default.asp?page_id=21387 (accessed April 4, 2010)

California State Parks; *Butterfield Overland Mail*; Internet publication; http://www.parks.ca.gov/?page_id=25444 (accessed Apr 27, 2010)

Conkling, Roscoe P. and Margaret B.; *The Butterfield Overland Mail, 1857–1869* (3 vols); Glendale, CA: A. H. Clark Company, 1947

Hoover, Mildred Brooke, Hero Eugene Rensch and Ethel Grace Rensch; *Historic Spots in California*; Stanford University Press; Stanford CA; 1932 (rev 1948)

National Park Service; *Juan Bautista de Anza National Historic Trail Guide Los Angeles County CA)*; Internet publication available at http://www.solideas.com/DeAnza/TrailGuide/Los_Angeles/index.html (accessed July 28, 2010)

Ormsby, Waterman L.; *The Butterfield Overland Mail (Only Through Passenger on the First Westbound Stage)*; original publications New York Herald (NY) Sep 26 - Nov 19, 1858; republished by Henry E. Huntington Library and Art Gallery, San Marino CA, 1942 - 1998

**Los Angeles Times / Mirror building - modern site
of 2nd Butterfield Station (N34.0529, W118.2447).
Photo by Fred Yeck (2008).**

Los Angeles to Campo de Cahuenga
April 27, 2011

Mirror Building / 1860 Butterfield Station - 145 S Spring Street; Los Angeles • Los Angeles County (N34° 3' 8.53", W118° 14' 42.00")

TO Campo de Cahuenga - 3919 Lankershim Boulevard; North Hollywood • Los Angeles County (N34° 8' 23.06", W118° 21' 42.68")

Approximate Actual Route Los Angeles to Campo de Cahuenga

10 miles.

(1858 Bailey itinerary says 12 miles; Ormsby says 9 miles.)

Notes:

The Butterfield Route from Los Angeles to Campo de Cahuenga appears to have roughly tracked modern US Highway 101 / Hollywood Freeway, slightly west of the de Anza route (1775-1776).

The next Butterfield Station at Campo de Cahuenga (coordinates N34° 8' 23.06", W118° 21' 42.68") has been an important site throughout the early history of California. Presently, it is a preserved historical site under the stewardship of the City of Los Angeles and the Campo de Cahuenga Historical Memorial Association. The site was purchased in 1923 by the City of Los Angeles. The Campo de Cahuenga Historical Memorial Association was formed in 1948.

In the early 1800s, Campo de Cahuenga was part of the Rancho Verdugo land grant owned by Mariano de la Luz Verdugo. In 1810 the San Fernando Mission took over Rancho Verdugo and the nearby Rancho Partezuela for cropland. The padres dammed the Los Angeles River near the Campo de Cahuenga site to irrigate fields. The mission administrators also built a small adobe that doubled as room for workers and for seed storage. By 1845 Tomas Feliz occupied the land and expanded the original building for his home to the size of the present building known as the Tomas Feliz Adobe by some, or the Cahuenga Adobe to others.

The present structure is a reproduction of the original Tomas Feliz Adobe. Kielbasa, in *Historic Adobes of Los Angeles County* writes, "The Cahuenga adobe was constructed in 1845 by Tomas Feliz at the north end of the pass bearing the same name. Cahuenga Pass was named for an ancient Indian village in the area and was the main passageway through the Hollywood Hills connecting Los Angeles and the San Fernando Valley. This well-traveled pass was the site of previous military engagements and subsequent peace negotiations. The revolt against Governor Manuel Victoria culminated here in 1831, and the famous Battle of Cahuenga was fought here in 1845, which resulted in the ouster of the unpopular governor, Manuel Micheltorena.

Tomas Feliz owned the Cahuenga Rancho where his modest six-room adobe stood. He was a member of the same family that owned neighboring Rancho Los Feliz, which today is the site of Griffith Park. It was on the "corredor" or the front porch of this adobe that Pico surrendered to Frémont in 1847 and the historic treaty was signed. The original English version of the Treaty of Cahuenga vanished without a trace; however, the original Spanish version was kept with General Pico at his San Fernando Mission home. This also disappeared, but was recovered seventy-four years later in the Bancroft Library in Berkeley, California, among the Pico family papers.

`The adobe of Tomas Feliz was allowed to decompose in time and was razed in 1900 due to road improvements along Lankershim Boulevard. On May 25, 1925, the City of Los Angeles purchased the site and kept it as a park commemorating the signing of the 1847 treaty. In 1950 an exact replica of the Cahuenga adobe was built by using old photographs and other documentation describing the house. The present building was placed on the exact site with the front door facing Lankershim Boulevard. It is a simple single story structure with a roof composed of red tiles."

According to information from the Campo de Cahuenga Historical Memorial Association:

> "The Campo de Cahuenga is the site of the 'Capitulation of Cahuenga,' an agreement that ended hostilities in California during the Mexican-American War. Also known as the 'Treaty of Cahuenga', these Articles of Capitulation were signed by American Lt. Col. John C. Fremont and Mexican General Andres Pico on January 13, 1847. The generous surrender terms allowed Pico's rebellious Californio insurgents to return to their ranchos and American military forces to prosecute the war further south in Mexico.

> The Capitulation secured the American occupation of California. The Campo de Cahuenga became known as the American 'Birthplace of California.' The Treaty of Guadalupe Hidalgo in 1848 formalized the annexation of California and the Southwest by the United States."

The historical association also notes:

> "It is located near the prehistoric Native American village of 'Kaweenga' (or 'Cahuenga'), on the northern entrance to the Cahuenga Pass. During the Spanish occupation of California (1769-1821), the El Camino Real passed by the Campo site on its way from the Pueblo of Los Angeles to the Mission San Fernando. The El Camino Real (King's Highway) connected all 21 missions, with presidios and pueblos during the Spanish period.

> The 1995 archaeological excavation of the site dates the original adobe construction sometime between 1797 and 1810. The Mission San Fernando constructed one of the largest adobes in

> Spanish California at the Campo. Located on an all-season ford of the Los Angeles River, we now believe it was used by the mission as headquarters for its extensive ranching operations."

The Campo de Cahuenga site is recognized with a California State Historical Sites marker (#151 Campo de Cahuenga). It reports "Here was made the Treaty of Cahuenga by General Andrés Pico, commanding forces for Mexico, and Lieutenant-Colonel J. C. Frémont, U.S. Army, for the United States. By this treaty, agreed upon January 13th, 1847, the United States acquired California - finally secured to us by the treaty of Guadalupe Hidalgo, made February 2nd, 1848. This legend was written February 9, 1898 by Mrs. Jessie Benton Frémont."

Campo de Cahuenga is listed on the National Register of Historic Places (2003 - #72001602)

Bailey and Ormsby specifically mention the Cahuenga Station. Hoover writes in some detail of the history of Campo de Cahuenga. Pittman mentions the location but does not speak to Butterfield significance.

References:

Bailey, Goddard; *California -- Arrival of the Overland Mail -- Itinerary of the Route*; as reported by newspaper article; New York Times (NY) - October 14, 1858

Bailey, Goddard; *Report to Postmaster General A.V. Brown - Full itinerary as reported by De Bow's Review and Industrial Resources, Statistics etc;* published by De Bow's Review; New Orleans and Washington City; 1858. See specifically *Internal Improvements - 1. Wagon Road to the Pacific*; pp 719-721. Internet accessible at http://books.google.com/books?id=5CYoAAAAYAAJ&pg=PA720&lpg=PA720&dq=Cienega+de+los+Pimas&source=bl&ots=_5lZw_Bq23&sig=T6scCb8cpbY7KwjxpYoNvZpcgvI&hl=en&ei=i6KnS6KNOIr2M5yprIED&sa=X&oi=book_result&ct=result&resnum=2&ved=_0CAwQ6AEwAQ#v=onepage&q=Cienega%20de%20los%20Pimas&f=false (accessed March 22, 2010)

California State Parks - Office of Historic Preservation; California Historical Landmarks; Internet database - http://www.parks.ca.gov/default.asp?page_id=21387 (accessed April 4, 2010)

Campo de Cahuenga Historical Memorial Association; *Campo de Cahuenga*; Internet publication accessible at http://www.campodecahuenga.com/ (accessed June 1, 2010)

Conkling, Roscoe P. and Margaret B.; *The Butterfield Overland Mail, 1857–1869* (3 vols); Glendale, CA: A. H. Clark Company, 1947

Hoover, Mildred Brooke, Hero Eugene Rensch and Ethel Grace Rensch; *Historic Spots in California*; Stanford University Press; Stanford CA; 1932 (rev 1948)

Kielbasa, John R.; *Historic Adobes of Los Angeles County*; Dorrance Publishing Co; Pittsburgh (July 1998); Internet publication (partial) - *Things to Do in Los Angeles*; http://www.laokay.com/halac/ (accessed March 9, 2010)

National Park Service; *Juan Bautista de Anza National Historic Trail Guide Los Angeles County CA)*; Internet publication at http://www.solideas.com/DeAnza/TrailGuide/Los_Angeles/index.html (accessed July 28, 2010)

Ormsby, Waterman L.; *The Butterfield Overland Mail (Only Through Passenger on the First Westbound Stage)*; original publications New York Herald (NY) Sep 26 - Nov 19, 1858; republished by Henry E. Huntington Library and Art Gallery, San Marino CA, 1942 - 1998

Pittman, Ruth; *Roadside History of California*; Mountain Press Publishing; Missoula MT; 1995

Restored adobe at Campo de Cahuenga
(N34.138, W118.363).
Photo by Fred Yeck (2008).

Campo de Cahuenga to Mission San Fernando Rey

April 27, 2011

Campo de Cahuenga - 3919 Lankershim Boulevard; North Hollywood • Los Angeles County (N34° 8' 23.06", W118° 21' 42.68")

TO Mission San Fernando Rey de España - 15151 San Fernando Mission Boulevard; Mission Hills • Los Angeles County (N34° 16' 21.92", W118° 27' 41.59")

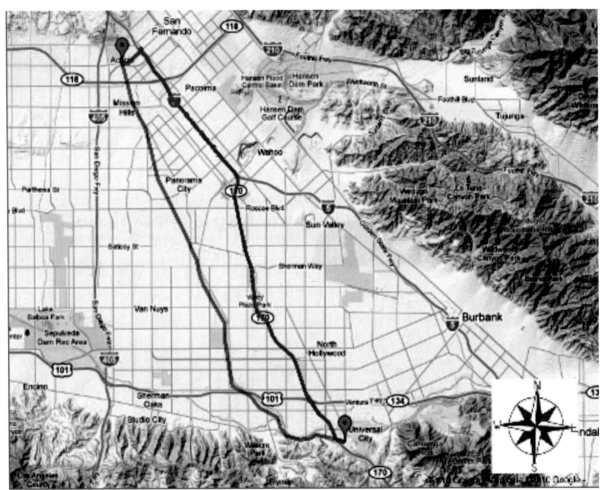

Approximate Actual Route Campo de Cahuenga to Mission San Fernando Rey de España - 10 miles.

(1858 Bailey itinerary says 12 miles; Ormsby says 15 miles)

Notes:

For lack of documented foundational research, the approximated original Butterfield Route through this segment is topographically derived, following a "path of least resistance" through the terrain along what would likely have been the 1858 version of the Old Mission Road / Camino Real.

This route skirts the western bank of the Los Angeles River tributary system through the relative flatlands between Studio City and San Fernando Rey. It has also been considered because it requires only one intermediate crossing on the Los Angeles River system rather than multiple crossings of various river tributaries.

Additional research is advisable for this route segment. It is likely that additional research during Butterfield Trail Planning and Implementation phases can more accurately pinpoint the specific original route.

The Mission of Fernando Rey de España (coordinates N34° 16' 21.92", W118° 27' 41.59") was established by Fray Fermin Francisco De Lasuén on September 8, 1797 as one of a chain of missions which were built to convert the native peoples to Christianity and to consolidate Spanish power along the coast of California.

According to information from the Archdiocese of Los Angeles, the Mission Church at this location is an exact replica of the original church which was built between 1804 and 1806. The walls of the church are seven feet thick at the base and five feet thick at the top. The material used was adobe brick and the people who built it were primarily the native peoples, who were called the Gabrieleños (Spanish name) or the Tongva Indians.

At one time the mission was a huge ranch with 121,542 acres of land. The mission padres raised as many as 21,745 cattle, sheep and horses and produced corn, wheat, tallow, soap, hides, shoes, cloth, wine, olive oil and ironwork. Woodwork, saddles and weaving were made in some of the workshops that can be seen there. The Convento was completed in 1822.

Today the mission is the Archival Center for the Catholic Church Archdiocese of Los Angeles.

The Mission San Fernando Rey was first established as a mission of the Catholic Church. In 1845, however, Mexican Governor Pío Pico declared the Mission buildings to be for sale. In 1846 he made the mission his headquarters. The mission served several functions while in private hands.

The Convento was the station for the Butterfield Stage Lines 1858-1861. It also served as a warehouse for the Porter Land and Water Company after that and, in 1896, a portion of the main mission square was used as a hog farm. San Fernando del Rey de España became a working church again in 1923.

The Hearst Foundation made a large bequest to the Mission in the 1940s which paid for substantial restorations. A 1971 earthquake severely damaged the church. Repairs were completed in 1974.

There is a California State Historical Sites marker at the Mission Convento (#157 -- Mission San Fernando del Rey de España). It reports "Mission San Fernando Rey de España was founded by Father Lasuén in September 8, 1797. A house belonging to Francisco Reyes, on Encino Rancho, furnished temporary shelter for the missionary in charge. An adobe chapel, built and blessed in December 1806, was damaged by the destructive earthquake of 1812 - a new church was completed in 1818".

The Mission is listed on the National Register of Historic Places (1988 - #88002147).

Bailey and Ormsby specifically mention the Mission San Fernando. Hoover and Pittman write extensively about the history of Mission San Fernando but do not speak directly to Butterfield significance.

References:

Bailey, Goddard; *California -- Arrival of the Overland Mail -- Itinerary of the Route*; as reported by newspaper article; New York Times (NY) - October 14, 1858

Bailey, Goddard; *Report to Postmaster General A.V. Brown - Full itinerary as reported by De Bow's Review and Industrial Resources, Statistics etc*; published by De Bow's Review; New Orleans and Washington City; 1858. See specifically *Internal Improvements - 1. Wagon Road to the Pacific*; pp 719-721. Internet accessible at http://books.google.com/books?id=5CYoAAAAYAAJ&pg=PA720&lpg=PA720&dq=Cienega+de+los+Pimas&source=bl&ots=_5lZw_Bq23&sig=T6scCb8cpbY7K wjxpYoNvZpcgvI&hl=en&ei=i6KnS6KNOIr2M5yprIED&sa=X&oi=book_result&ct=result&resnum=2&ved=_0CAwQ6AEwAQ#v=onepage&q=Cienega%20de%20los%20Pimas&f=false (accessed March 22, 2010)

California State Parks - Office of Historic Preservation; California Historical Landmarks; Internet database -

http://www.parks.ca.gov/default.asp?page_id=21387 (accessed April 4, 2010)

Conkling, Roscoe P. and Margaret B.; *The Butterfield Overland Mail, 1857–1869* (3 vols); Glendale, CA: A. H. Clark Company, 1947

Hoover, Mildred Brooke, Hero Eugene Rensch and Ethel Grace Rensch; *Historic Spots in California*; Stanford University Press; Stanford CA; 1932 (rev 1948)

National Register of Historic Places; *National Register Locations by State*; Internet publication; accessible at

http://www.nationalregisterofhistoricplaces.com/state.html (accessed May 3, 2010)

Ormsby, Waterman L.; *The Butterfield Overland Mail (Only Through Passenger on the First Westbound Stage)*; original publications New York Herald (NY) Sep 26 - Nov 19, 1858; republished by Henry E. Huntington Library and Art Gallery, San Marino CA, 1942 - 1998

Pittman, Ruth; *Roadside History of California*; Mountain Press Publishing; Missoula MT; 1995

**Mission San Ferando Rey de Espana
(N34.273, W118.462).
Photo by Fred Yeck (2008).**

Mission San Fernando Rey to Hart's Station

April 27, 2011

Mission San Fernando Rey de España - 15151 San Fernando Mission Boulevard; Mission Hills • Los Angeles County (N34° 16' 21.92", W118° 27' 41.59")

TO Hart's (Lyons') Station - 23287 N Sierra Highway; Newhall • Los Angeles County (N34° 21' 45.04", W118° 30' 25.81")

Approximate Actual Route Mission San Fernando Rey de España to Hart's Station - 7.7 miles.

(1858 Bailey itinerary says 8 miles)

Secondary Landmarks:

Beale's Cut - near Antelope Valley Freeway, Newhall CA - N34° 20' 31.68", W118° 30' 34.26"

Hart's Station (possible alternative) – vicinity of Sierra Highway and Newhall Avenue (Newhall CA)

Notes:

Some additional study is advised to more accurately determine the specific Butterfield Overland Route northward from the Mission San Fernando Rey de Espana. From this segment onward to about Gilroy CA, the Butterfield Route diverged from the old Spanish routes into trails established toward the gold camps and settlements of the '49ers (1849).

This "gold camp route" was used by an earlier local stageline established by Phineas Banning in 1854 and continued to be used by Banning after the Butterfield Southern / Ox Bow Route shut down in 1861. Additional study of the Banning Line should be helpful in more precisely defining these routes.

Modern / local research indicates the route essentially tracked along the present route of the Golden State Freeway through this area and into the vicinity of the Antelope Valley Freeway.

From the intersection of the two freeways, the route into Santa Clarita / Newhall CA can be accurately placed passing to the west of the Antelope Valley Freeway.

As a specific landmark locating the leg approaching Hart's Station, there is an intermediate landmark that has come to be known as "Beale's Cut" (approximate coordinates N34° 20' 31.68", W118° 30' 34.26")

One of the main obstacles to travel north from Los Angeles was the rugged, barely passable mountain pass between the Santa Clarita and San Fernando valleys. In the early 1800s, Henry Clay Wiley came up with a unique solution at this pass. In partnership with Ygnacio del Valle, Wiley built a massive wooden windlass that operated like a huge elevator. The structure served to raise and lower wagons, animals and people over the steep incline. Wiley and del Valle also built a thriving inn nearby, known as Wiley Station to serve the travelers awaiting their turn on the "elevator."

In 1854, Phineas Banning leveled and deepened the pass to accommodate his stage and freight services, rather than awaiting the "elevator" every time.

Come 1863, General Edward Fitzgerald Beale and a contingent of soldiers deepened the cut by an additional 60 feet and moderated the grade into the pass.

"Beale's Cut" operated as a toll road until 1886 and was the only passage north out of Los Angeles until the nearby Newhall Tunnel opened in 1910. The tunnel, in turn, was dug out to form a pass during the realignment of California Highway 6 in 1938.

Hoover mentions "Beal Cut" only in passing - placing it at the southern entrance to Newhall Pass.

As to Hart's Station proper, twin brothers Sanford and Cyrus Lyon purchased the aforementioned Wiley Station in 1855, which remained successful despite lost revenues from the no-longer-necessary "elevator." According to local historian A.B. Perkins, "Lyons' Station" is synonymous with what Ormsby and Bailey identified as "Hart's Station" or "Hart's Ranch".

No sketches or photographs of Lyons' Station have surfaced. However, Perkins reports an 1875 description as follows:

> "The station proper is a well-constructed frame building about 30x60 feet, answering the purpose of a store, post office, telegraph office, depot and tavern, being altogether the head center of the adjacent valley.
>
> Besides this, there is a large stable, and back towards the foothills on the West (the Needham ranch, just north of the cemetery), a little cottage half hid by a grove of Mountain Oak."

There is a California Historic Sites marker (#688 Lyons' Stagecoach Stop) at the former location of Lyons' Station -- which is now the site of the Eternal Valley Memorial Park cemetery (coordinates N34° 21' 45.04", W118° 30' 25.81"). That marker says, "This site was the location of a combination store, post office, telegraph office, tavern, and stage depot accommodating travelers during the Kern River gold rush in the early 1850s. A regular stop for Butterfield and other early California stage lines, it was purchased by Sanford and Cyrus Lyons in 1855, and by 1868 at least twenty families lived here. Eternal Valley Memorial Park has called their final resting place 'The Garden of the Pioneers'".

Waterman Ormsby refers to the station, noting that "Eight miles from San Fernando (Mission) we changed horses again at Hart's Ranch, having made nearly ten miles per hour in spite of the bad condition of the roads after one of the heaviest rains ever known in the county."

Bailey also notes "Hart's" as being eight miles from Mission San Fernando.

While there is no known record of a "Hart" owning the station. It is quite possible that a "Hart" was the station attendant or manager at the time of Ormsby's and Bailey's trips. Perkins notes that "Its name changed with that of the current stage-tender, or station operator. It was known variously as Fountain's, Hart's, Hosmer's, Andrews', Lyons' at various dates."

Some local research indicates that the location of "Hart's Ranch" may have been slightly north of the Eternal Valley historical marker location -- in the vicinity of Sierra Highway and Newhall Avenue, Newhall CA. That location is approximately 475 yards north of the Eternal Valley marker.

References:

Bailey, Goddard; *California -- Arrival of the Overland Mail -- Itinerary of the Route*; as reported by newspaper article; New York Times (NY) - October 14, 1858

Bailey, Goddard; *Report to Postmaster General A.V. Brown - Full itinerary as reported by De Bow's Review and Industrial Resources, Statistics etc*; published by De Bow's Review; New Orleans and Washington City; 1858. See specifically *Internal Improvements - 1. Wagon Road to the Pacific*; pp 719-721. Internet accessible at http://books.google.com/books?id=5CYoAAAAYAAJ&pg=PA720&lpg=PA720& dq=Cienega+de+los+Pimas&source=bl&ots=_5lZw_Bq23&sig=T6scCb8cpbY7K wjxpYoNvZpcgvI&hl=en&ei=i6KnS6KNOIr2M5yprIED&sa=X&oi=book_result& ct=result&resnum=2&ved=__0CAwQ6AEwAQ#v=onepage&q=Cienega%20de% 20los%20Pimas&f=false (accessed March 22, 2010)

California State Parks - Office of Historic Preservation; California Historical Landmarks; Internet database - http://www.parks.ca.gov/default.asp?page_id=21387 (accessed April 4, 2010)

Conkling, Roscoe P. and Margaret B.; *The Butterfield Overland Mail, 1857–1869* (3 vols); Glendale, CA: A. H. Clark Company, 1947

Hoover, Mildred Brooke, Hero Eugene Rensch and Ethel Grace Rensch; *Historic Spots in California*; Stanford University Press; Stanford CA; 1932 (rev 1948)

Ormsby, Waterman L.; *The Butterfield Overland Mail (Only Through Passenger on the First Westbound Stage)*; original publications New York Herald (NY) Sep 26 - Nov 19, 1858; republished by Henry E. Huntington Library and Art Gallery, San Marino CA, 1942 - 1998

Perkins, A.B.; *Santa Clarita Valley in Pictures - Early Transportation*; Santa Clarita Valley Historical Society; Internet publication accessible at http://www.scvhistory.com/scvhistory/signal/perkins/part04.html (accessed June 1, 2010)

**Modern vicinity of Hart's Station, Newhall CA
(N34.363, W118.507).
Photo by Fred Yeck (2008).**

Hart's Station to King's Station

April 27, 2011

Hart's (Lyons') Station - 23287 N Sierra Highway; Newhall • Los Angeles County (N34° 21' 45.04", W118° 30' 25.81")

TO King's Station (approximate by mileage) - Drinkwater Canyon • Los Angeles County (N34° 31' 37.44", W118° 31' 54.41")

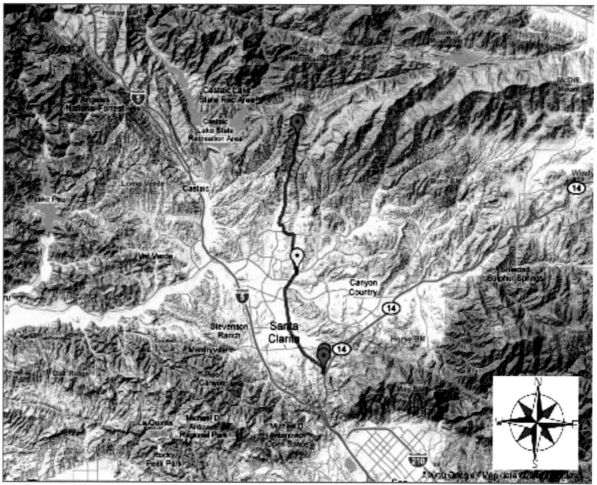

Approximate Actual Route Hart's Station to King's Station

13.3 miles.

(1858 Bailey itinerary says 12 miles)

Secondary Landmarks:

Casa de Martin Ruiz - approximate coordinates N34° 25' 58.89", W118° 31' 53.49"

Notes:

Here again, the continuing Butterfield Route appears to have followed an earlier Banning Stagelines Route (1854), although the next few Butterfield stops have almost disappeared into history.

Contemporaneous mileage estimates of the Butterfield Route (1858) compared to 20th Century local research allow historians to make a good comparative track, but not all of the listed Butterfield stops can be definitively sited.

Historical accounts indicate that the Butterfield route followed the San Francisquito Canyon before surmounting the head of the canyon and turning westward toward Fort Tejon and into Grapevine Canyon.

Local historian Jerry Reynolds, for example, notes that "Ever since the days of Phineas Banning, General Beale and the Butterfield Overland stage, vehicles made their way out of Los Angeles, through San Francisquito Canyon, down the Grapevine Pass, and then into Bakersfield. The California Highway Commission was formed in 1911, and one of its first priorities was to build a simpler, more direct road through the La Liebre Mountains."

That "simpler, more direct route" is the "Ridge Route" generally followed by the present Interstate 5 but impassable for the Butterfield coaches. Researcher Harrison Irving Scott, in his book *Ridge Route - The Road That United California*, writes in general terms of the route through this area during the Butterfield period.

Hoover's *Historic Spots in California* contains several paragraphs describing various stage stations in this segment, all of which are on the San Francisquito / Tejon Pass / Grapevine Canyon route. Unfortunately, the names she cites for these stations do not jibe with the accounts by Bailey or other researchers and some appear to be post-Butterfield. Neither does Hoover include precise locations for the locations to which she refers.

Hoover's *Historic Spots in California* mentions only two station possibilities in this area. One of those (Casa de Martin Ruiz) is worth mention even if unlikely, being only about 6 miles from Lyons (north of "Bouquet Junction" at the intersection of Bouquet Canyon Road and Seco Canyon Road; approximate coordinates N34° 25' 58.89", W118° 31' 53.49").

Says Hoover, "La Casa de Martin Ruiz is the last of several adobe homes built by Martin Ruiz and his sons in the Canyon del Buque (erroneously called 'Bouquet Canyon' by General Beale and other early topographers). It was in this same region that Francisco or 'Chico' Lopez, discoverer of gold in Placeritos Canyon, pastured his cattle during the '40s and where Francisco Chari, one of his herdsmen, later took upland [nearby]. Chari was a French sailor whom the Californians nicknamed 'El Buque' (Spanish for 'The Ship') because of his many tales of the sea and of the ships in which he sailed. Ruiz sold the rancho to Battista Suraco, a Genoan, in 1874. Facing west, the surviving adobe (in 1932) stands a mile or two up the canyon at the point where it widens into a narrow valley. A modern road runs about ten feet from the back door. The low, rambling one story building has been long neglected and is rapidly crumbling under the inroads of the elements."

Kielbasa's *Historic Adobes of Los Angeles County* also mentions the "Francisco Chari Adobe (Rancho Del Buque) Est. 1843" but notes only that "Chari was a French sailor who jumped ship and became a Mexican citizen. He established Rancho Del Buque (Ship Ranch) which would later be misspelled as Bouquet Canyon, changing the name from 'boat' to 'flowers.'" No firm location information is listed in Kielbasa's listing for the Chari Adobe.

Hoover's *Historic Spots In California* also mentions that "Major Gordon's Stage Post is one old adobe still standing in San Francisquito Canyon." But that's all she wrote -- literally. There are no specifics that would accurately place "Major Gordon's" adobe. Unfortunately, Hoover offers no elaboration as to who "Major Gordon" may have been.

As to the listed King's Station location, it would be nice to say this area was chosen for reasons other than the fact that it is a wide spot in the road. Unfortunately, that is barely the case. By Bailey's measurements, King's was 12 miles from Hart's / Lyons'. An even 12-mile draw along San Francisquito Canyon would put the station in a rather thin area of the canyon which is not likely as a station site. The next nearest wide spot is only 10 miles from Lyons', making it unlikely given the mileage estimates. The site approximated in this report lies 13.3 miles from Hart's -- which can be sited fairly specifically.

It should also be noted that the local name for this area ("Drinkwater Canyon") is likely to have denoted a spot where one could have obtained a drink of water -- assuming (as is likely in this area) that "Drinkwater Canyon" is a name dating from the Butterfield period or earlier.

Ormsby specifically places the route through this segment being via the San Francisquito Canyon. Bailey specifically notes the station as "King's," but no further details are presently available about either the station location or its namesake.

The Conklings mention that an alternate name for King's was Hollandsville; however, no additional information has been found regarding a location in this area by that name.

It is probable that more information regarding the routing and placement of this site can be found during Butterfield Trail Route Planning and Implementation phases given additional research with and assistance from the Santa Clarita Valley Historical Society and Angeles National Forest personnel.

• Data update as of April 2013 • Researcher Fred Yeck places King's Station at coordinates N34° 32' 0.24", W118° 31' 41.88", slightly northeast of these report coordinates. Researchers with the Santa Clarita Valley Historical Association have indicated that King's Station may have been slightly northeast of the report coordinates as well. A definitive answer may never be known, however, as the site was demolished in 1928 during disastrous flooding when the Saint Francis Dam failed and inundated the entire area.

References:

Bailey, Goddard; *California -- Arrival of the Overland Mail -- Itinerary of the Route*; as reported by newspaper article; New York Times (NY) - October 14, 1858

Bailey, Goddard; *Report to Postmaster General A.V. Brown - Full itinerary as reported by De Bow's Review and Industrial Resources, Statistics etc;* published by De Bow's Review; New Orleans and Washington City; 1858. See specifically *Internal Improvements - 1. Wagon Road to the Pacific*; pp 719-721. Internet accessible at http://books.google.com/books?id=5CYoAAAAYAAJ&pg=PA720&lpg=PA720& dq=Cienega+de+los+Pimas&source=bl&ots=_5lZw_Bq23&sig=T6scCb8cpbY7K wjxpYoNvZpcgvI&hl=en&ei=i6KnS6KNOIr2M5yprIED&sa=X&oi=book_result& ct=result&resnum=2&ved=__0CAwQ6AEwAQ#v=onepage&q=Cienega%20de% 20los%20Pimas&f=false (accessed March 22, 2010)

Conkling, Roscoe P. and Margaret B.; *The Butterfield Overland Mail, 1857–1869* (3 vols); Glendale, CA: A. H. Clark Company, 1947

Hoover, Mildred Brooke, Hero Eugene Rensch and Ethel Grace Rensch; *Historic Spots in California*; Stanford University Press; Stanford CA; 1932 (rev 1948)

Kielbasa, John R.; *Historic Adobes of Los Angeles County*; Dorrance Publishing Co; Pittsburgh (July 1998); Internet publication (partial) Things to Do in Los Angeles; http://www.laokay.com/halac/ (accessed March 9, 2010)

Ormsby, Waterman L.; *The Butterfield Overland Mail (Only Through Passenger on the First Westbound Stage)*; original publications New York Herald (NY) Sep 26 - Nov 19, 1858; republished by Henry E. Huntington Library and Art Gallery, San Marino CA, 1942 - 1998

Reynolds, Jerry; *Santa Clarita Valley in Pictures - Grapevine Grade*; Santa Clarita Valley Historical Society; Internet publication accessible at http://www.scvhistory.com/scvhistory/lw2021.htm (accessed June 1, 2010)

Scott, Harrison Irving; *Ridge Route - The Road That United California*, published by the author; Torrance CA; 2002

**Vicinity of King's Station
(N34.534, W118.525).
Photo by Fred Yeck (2008).**

King's Station to Widow Smith's Station

January 14, 2012

King's Station (approximate by mileage) - Drinkwater Canyon • Los Angeles County (N34° 31' 37.44", W118° 31' 54.41")

TO Widow Smith's - 38839 San Francisquito Canyon Road - near Green Valley • Los Angeles County (N34° 36' 52.84", W118° 25' 37.28")

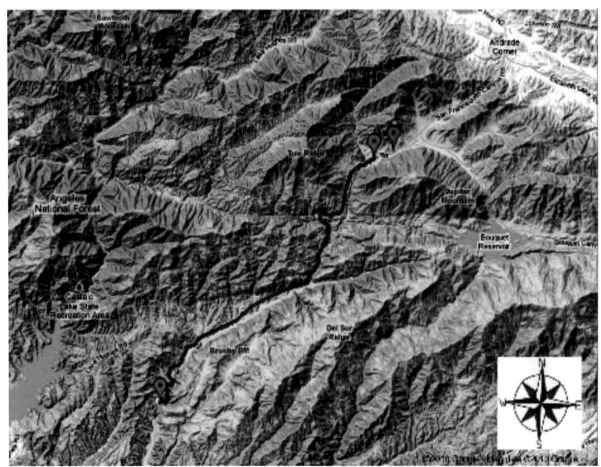

Approximate Actual Route, King's Station to Widow Smith's

Station 10.2 miles (1858 Bailey itinerary says 10 miles)

Secondary Landmarks:

Butterfield Stage Historical Marker per Fred Yeck – near intersection of San Francisquito Canyon Road at Pelton Street (coordinates N34.580, W118.459 N34° 34' 48.00", W118° 27' 32.40"

"Old Adobe Stage Stop" (Widow Smith Station? per Kielbasa) - 38839 San Francisquito Canyon Road - coordinates N34° 36' 55.76", W118° 25' 36.30"

Widow Smith site based upon Bailey mileage - N34 36' 45.06", W118 26' 07.90"

Widow Smith site based upon Fred Yeck / Conkling description coordinates - N34° 37' 19.20", W118° 24' 46.80"

Notes:

The Butterfield Route through this segment continued on an essentially northerly course through the San Francisquito Canyon and appears to have followed the 1854 Banning Stage Route. Little is known about the specific route location in this area. However, the topography is such that the route can be ascertained to a fairly specific degree and appears to have followed the existing San Francisquito Canyon Road.

Information from Butterfield researcher Fred Yeck of Tucson AZ cites the Conklings' description of the route and station site as follows: "... the road followed along the bottom of the canyon, and about two and a half miles from the station passed through the most constricted part of the gorge, where sixty-five years later the St. Francis dam was constructed, and which collapsed in the winter of 1928, when four hun-dred lives were lost and seven hundred homes were swept away. About 6 miles farther on, the road left the bottom and took a course along the higher ground on the west side of the canyon for two miles and a half to Widow Smith's or as it appears to have become later known as Clayton's, the next station eleven miles north of King's...".

Yeck also noted the discovery of a Butterfield-related historical marker "at Pelton Road near Powerhouse # 1" which he cited by GPS during a visit to the area at coordinates N34° 34' 48.00", W118° 27' 32.40".

Initially, the exact location of the Widow Smith Station was somewhat inexact. Route mileage based upon Bailey's notation did not exactly agree with the Conklings' later placement of the station site. Those disagreements, however, have been resolved as of January 2012.

Initial findings based upon Bailey's mileage to the next eastward station (King's) compared to the known route rendered an approximation of the Widow Smith site at coordinates N34 36' 45.06", W118 26' 07.90" while Yeck's findings (based upon the Conklings' description of the site) placed the site approximately 1.5 miles to the north at coordinates N34° 37' 19.20", W118° 24' 46.80".

In his research, Kielbasa (1998) indicates that this station was probably located in the vicinity of 38839 San Francisquito Canyon Road (coordinates N34° 36' 55.76", W118° 25' 36.30"). In *Historic Adobes of Los Angeles County,* he notes the location of an unnamed "Old Adobe Stage Stop" – which site represented an intermediate point between the initially approximated site and the site as estimated by Yeck.

Kielbasa writes of this location as "Two miles west of Green Valley. It served as a stage stop when the Butterfield Stage passed this way from 1858 to 1861. It stood until the 1960s. It was torn down, but a later two-story adobe stands next to the site and is still occupied."

In a March, 2010 telephone interview, Pat Saletero of the Santa Clarita Valley Historical Society indicated that the location of Widow Smith's Station is known. She could not cite the precise location, but seemed to indicate that it was slightly south of Kielbasa's location. During follow-up discussions as of January, 2012, Saletero supplied a roadside photograph of the Widow Smith location via Google Maps clearly indicating the station site at coordinates N34° 36' 52.84", W118° 25' 37.28". The Saletero site is approximately 200 feet from the Kielbasa site – clearly substantiating the findings by Kielbasa. For the purpose of this report, the specific co-ordinates for the Saletero site have been used o identify the Widow Smith station site.

Saletero also noted that remnants of the original structure may remain or have been incorporated into the present structure.

No specific information has been found regarding "Widow Smith". It is possible, however that additional interpretive information might be discovered during Butterfield Overland Trail Planning and Implementation phases. Once again, the Santa Clarita Valley Historical Society has been helpful and has expressed interest in assisting with further research.

Ormsby does not specifically mention Widow Smith's. Bailey, however, cites it as a mileage point.

The Conklings state that this station may have been called Clayton in later years – although no further details are available. In addition, they note that "the names of two others, John F. Gordon, and a Mr. Wilburn" were also associated with this station. No additional information has been fund regarding either Gordon or Wilburn. Gudde's *California Place Names: The Origin and Etymology of Current Geographical Names* includes an entry for "Clayton." That entry; however, indicates the location to have been in Contra Costa County near Mount Diablo – approximately 360 miles northwest of this section of the San Francisquito Canyon.

This route segment appears to be wholly within the Angeles National Forest. It is quite possible that additional consultation with personnel from Los Padres National Forest would help to further confirm the routing and the Widow Smith Station site.

References:

Bailey, Goddard; *California -- Arrival of the Overland Mail -- Itinerary of the Route*; as reported by newspaper article; *New York Times* (NY) - October 14, 1858.

Bailey, Goddard; *Report to Postmaster A.V. Brown - Full itinerary as reported by De Bow's Review and Industrial Resources, Statistics etc*; published by De Bow's Review; New Orleans and Washington City; 1858. See specifically *Internal Improvements - 1. Wagon Road to the Pacific*; pp 719-721. Internet accessible at http://books.google.com/books?id=5CYoAAAAYAAJ&pg=PA720&lpg=PA720&dq=Cienega+de+los+Pimas&source=bl&ots=_5lZw_Bq23&sig=T6scCb8cpbY7K wjxpYoNvZpcgvI&hl=en&ei=i6KnS6KNOIr2M5yprIED&sa=X&oi=book_result&ct=result&resnum=2&ved=_0CAwQ6AEwAQ#v=onepage&q=Cienega%20de%20los%20Pimas&f=false (accessed March 22, 2010).

Conkling, Roscoe P. and Margaret B.; *The Butterfield Overland Mail, 1857–1869* (3 vols.); Glendale, CA: A. H. Clark Company, 1947.

Gudde, Irwin Gustav; *California Place Names: The Origin and Etymology of Current Geographical Names*; University of California Press; 1998.

Kielbasa, John R.; *Historic Adobes of Los Angeles County*; Dorrance Publishing Co; Pittsburgh (July 1998); Internet publication (partial) Things to Do in Los Angeles; http://www.laokay.com/halac/ (accessed March 9, 2010).

Ormsby, Waterman L.; *The Butterfield Overland Mail (Only Through Passenger on the First Westbound Stage)*; original publications *New York Herald* (NY) Sep 26 - Nov 19, 1858; republished by Henry E. Huntington Library and Art Gallery, San Marino CA, 1942 – 1998.

Yeck, Fred; *The Butterfield Overland Mail;* 2011 – unpublished monograph supplied by the author.

Butterfield sign, Patton Rd., near Widow Smith Station (N34.580, W118.459).
Photo by Fred Yeck (2008).

Widow Smith's Station to French John's Station

January 14, 2012

Widow Smith's - 38839 San Francisquito Canyon Road - near Green Valley • Los Angeles County (N34° 36' 52.84", W118° 25' 37.28")

TO French John's / Cow Springs - near Neenach, CA • Los Angeles County (N34° 46' 21.83", W118° 37' 16.82")

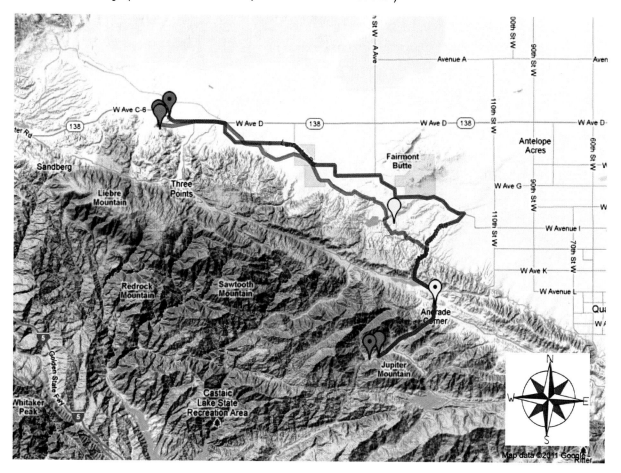

Approximate Actual Route, Widow Smith's to French John's

24 miles (1858 Bailey itinerary says 24 miles)

Secondary Landmarks:

La Casa de Miguel Ortiz - 13980 Elizabeth Lake Road - coordinates N34° 39' 06.75", W118° 22' 36.79"

Mud Springs Station per Yeck / Conklings – coordinates N34° 42' 21.60", W118° 24' 50.40"

Notes:

The continuing Butterfield Route represents the point at which the essentially northward route through the San Francisquito Canyon entered the westerly course toward Grapevine Canyon -- again along the 1854 Banning Stage Route. There is some confusion along this route in that some historical maps indicate a westward road via Pine Canyon (modern Pine Canyon Road) from the area near Elizabeth Lake while other research indicates the route of 1858 as having continued northward into the Antelope Valley via what is now Muniz Ranch Road before turning westward following a riverside course in the vicinity of what is now Lancaster Road. It now appears most likely that the Butterfield Route followed this Antelope Valley route rather than the Pine Valley.

`While possibly post-Butterfield, there is an interesting intermediate location approximately four miles north of the "Widow Smith's" site that helps to locate the route. Kielbasa and Hoover both speak of La Casa de Miguel Ortiz as a known stage stop (13980 Elizabeth Lake Road, coordinates N34° 39' 06.75", W118° 22' 36.79"). Some local residents report this location as being nearer to 14021 Elizabeth Lake Road – approximately 300 feet from the Kielbasa site.

La Casa de Miguel Ortiz stands just south of the modern T-intersection of San Francisquito Canyon Road and Elizabeth Lake Road.

Says Kielbasa, "This lengthy single story adobe casa stands at 13980 Elizabeth Lake Road. It was situated along the old stage road, which ascended from San Francisquito Canyon. It was the home of Miguel Ortiz, who was employed by General Edward F. Beale as a muleteer. Ortiz built this adobe home on land given to him by Beale. It was part of Rancho La Liebre and was approximately eighteen miles [southeast] of Beale's adobe hacienda. At one time, Miguel Leonis owned land in the Elizabeth Lake region. In the 1870s, the area was frequented by the *bandido*, Tiburcio Vasquez. This house is a private residence and not open to the public."

Hoover notes that "It is said to have been the first building erected at the lake [Elizabeth Lake] and was built by Miguel Ortiz, a muleteer, who was in the employ of General Beale. The land was given him by the General."

Neither Kielbasa nor Hoover specifically date the construction of Casa Miguel Ortiz.

The Conklings also noted a specific intermediary Butterfield station as of 1859 between Widow Smith and French John's: "...Mud Springs, the next station thirteen miles northwest of Widow Smith's... established about December 1858, to provide a relay team on the twenty-seven mile stage between Widow Smith's and French John's". Until recently, however, it has been difficult to place this site.

Researcher Fred Yeck (following the Conklings' description) notes that recent DeLorme computer mapping identifies a site known as Mud Springs at coordinates N34° 42' 21.60", W118° 24' 50.40" (N34.706, W118.414) in this area. In his monograph The Butterfield Overland Mail (2011), Yeck noted "... we found Mud Springs located on the DeLorme Southern California Gazetteer at N34.708, W118.414, east of Fairmont Reservoir. This segment measured only 8 miles, not the 13 claimed by Conkling, but the distances before and after this segment are correct, so maybe they needed to take an indirect route from Widow Smith's to Mud Spring for some reason. This is right near the California Aqueduct where it dives under a small river."

In a telephone interview as of January 2011, local researcher Harrison Irving Scott (author of Ridge Route - The Road That United California, 2002) noted that he was aware of a "Mud Springs" location along the early stage route but was unable to site it exactly. Similarly, Bonnie Ketterl Kane of the Ridge Route Communities Historical Society (Frazier Park CA) confirmed knowledge of a "Mud Springs Station" but was unable to place it exactly.

In January of 2012, however, Kane and Scott both concurred with Yeck's finding that the Mud Springs site was likely to have been in the vicinity of Yeck's location at N34° 42' 21.60", W118° 24' 50.40" and that the Antelope Valley route for the Butterfield was the most likely.

Yeck's coordinates appear to place the Mud Springs site on or near property of the Antelope Valley Sportsman's Club. It is likely that consultation with the Antelope Valley Sportsman's Club might help to more closely identify this site.

Very little is known of this station specifically and neither Ormsby nor Bailey mention it in their writings.

Regarding "French John's", no specific site for this station could be located, although some references (including Conklings) refer to it as having been at "Cow Springs"). Specifically, the Conklings noted "... French John's or Cow spring, as the next station fourteen miles northwest from Mud Springs became later known ... The site of French John's is a mile and an eight southwest of Neenach."

The descriptions of "French John's" appear to place it in the vicinity of the later residence of General Edward F. Beale on his "Rancho La Liebre" (Jackrabbit Ranch), although there is no particular "French connection" to be found other than the translation of "liebre" from the French to English as "hare" or "rabbit."

Kielbasa says:

> In 1855, Beale purchased Rancho La Liebre for a mere three cents an acre. The 48,799 acre rancho was originally granted to Jose Maria Flores on April 21, 1846, by Governor Pio Pico. Flores was the commander and chief of the Mexican forces in California during the Mexican War. Flores nearly lost his entitlement to the rancho when the U.S. Land Commission declared the grant to be fraudulently obtained. The Land Commission contended that Pico backdated many of the land grants he issued and that Rancho La Liebre was granted while California was under American control and no longer a part of Mexico. However, Flores won an appeal and kept the title.

> Rancho La Liebre was named as such because of the abundance of jackrabbits in the area. The rancho was mostly comprised of mountainous terrain. It was in the northwest part of the Los Angeles County and lay to the west of Antelope Valley. By the time Beale acquired La Liebre, he had married Mary Edwards and had a son named Truxtun. Beale built an adobe home for his wife on the rancho. This sturdy and roomy adobe house was constructed in Canon de las Osas (Bear Canyon) at the western edge of Antelope Valley. Beale ran sheep on the rancho with Robert S. Baker, who would later become one of the founders of Santa Monica, California. Their flocks grew to over 100,000 head. After obtaining possession of La Liebre, Beale allowed Don Andres Pico and his son, Romulo, to graze their own flocks of sheep at the southeast part of the rancho. This was the same Andres Pico who was Beale's enemy at the Battle of San Pasqual. The two men became friends and eventually business associates.

Hoover's *Historic Spots in California* speaks specifically of Beale having built a residence at the location "in the early '60s."

Here again, Yeck followed the Conklings' description of the location and located several unidentified small springs on DeLorme mapping at coordinates N34° 46' 12.00", W118° 37' 12.00". Specifically, Yeck noted "The town of Neenach is just north of Lancaster Road. Searching its history we learned that the Neenach school was one mile northeast of Cow Spring. We found the school about three-quarters of a mile north of Lancaster Road on 270th Street. Measuring back 1-1/8 miles from the school we found a store on Lancaster Road at N34.783, W118.628. The De Lorme Gazetteer shows "Springs" about a half mile south of this store. This would be the location of Cow Spring and French John's Station at N34.7732, W118.6215".

During a March, 2010, telephone interview, Bonnie Ketterl Kane of the Ridge Route Communities Museum and Historical Society (Frazier Park CA) indicated that the actual French John's site may have been in the vicinity later noted by Yeck but was unable to place it exactly. During follow-up correspondence as of January 2012, however, Kane identified a satellite image of the Cow Springs / French John site at coordinates N34° 46' 21.83", W118° 37' 16.82" (approximately 1100 feet northwest of Yeck's coordinates for the unidentified springs on the DeLorme maps).

It should also be noted that information from the Tejon Ranch development company indicates that Rancho La Liebre was one of the cornerstone properties of what would become the Tejon Ranch as of 1855. Additionally, further consultation is recommended with the Antelope Valley Sportsmans' Club and the West Antelope Valley Historical Society (Lancaster CA).

Ormsby describes his travel through this area but does not specifically mention "French John's." Bailey specifies the station as a mileage point.

References:

Bailey, Goddard; *California -- Arrival of the Overland Mail -- Itinerary of the Route*; as reported by newspaper article; *New York Times* (NY) - October 14, 1858.

Bailey, Goddard; *Report to Postmaster General A.V. Brown - Full itinerary as reported by De Bow's Review and Industrial Resources, Statistics etc;* published by De Bow's Review; New Orleans and Washington City; 1858. See specifically *Internal Improvements - 1. Wagon Road to the Pacific*; pp 719-721. Internet accessible at http://books.google.com/books?id=5CYoAAAAYAAJ&pg=PA720&lpg=PA720&dq=Cienega+de+los+Pimas&source=bl&ots=_5lZw_Bq23&sig=T6scCb8cpbY7KwjxpYoNvZpcgvI&hl=en&ei=i6KnS6KNOIr2M5yprIED&sa=X&oi=book_result&ct=result&resnum=2&ved=_0CAwQ6AEwAQ#v=onepage&q=Cienega%20de%20los%20Pimas&f=false (accessed March 22, 2010).

Conkling, Roscoe P. and Margaret B.; *The Butterfield Overland Mail, 1857–1869* (3 vols.); Glendale, CA: A. H. Clark Company, 1947.

Kielbasa, John R.; *Historic Adobes of Los Angeles County*; Dorrance Publishing Co; Pittsburgh (July 1998); Internet publication (partial) Things to Do in Los Angeles; http://www.laokay.com/halac/ (accessed March 9, 2010).

Ormsby, Waterman L.; *The Butterfield Overland Mail (Only Through Passenger on the First Westbound Stage)*; original publications *New York Herald* (NY) Sep 26 - Nov 19, 1858; republished by Henry E. Huntington Library and Art Gallery, San Marino CA, 1942 - 1998.

Scott, Harrison Irving; *Ridge Route - The Road That United California*, published by the author; Torrance CA; 2002

Tejon Ranch Company; *Conservation Timeline 1850 - 1874*; Internet publication accessible at http://www.tejonranch.com/conservation/timeline.asp (accessed June 4, 2010).

Yeck, Fred; *The Butterfield Overland Mail*; 2011 – unpublished monograph supplied by the author.

French John's Station to Reed's Ranch

January 14, 2012

French John's / Cow Springs - near Neenach, CA • Los Angeles County (N34° 46' 21.83", W118° 37' 16.82")

Reed's Ranch - Gorman • Los Angeles County (N34° 47' 48.88", W118° 51' 28.31")

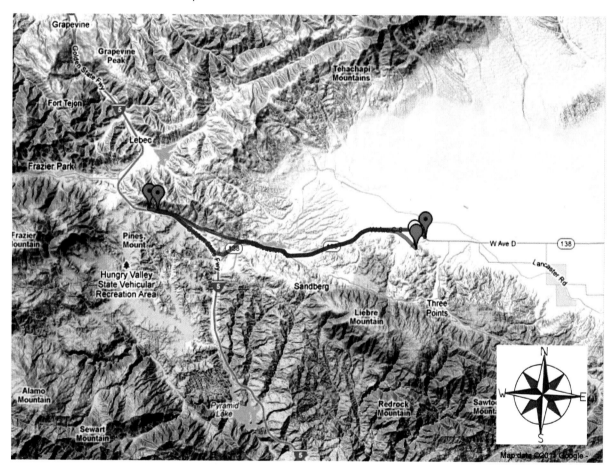

Approximate Actual Route, French John's to Reed's Ranch

14 miles (1858 Bailey itinerary says 14 miles)

Secondary Landmarks:

Reed's ranch per Kane and Scott - vicinity of 49669 Gorman Post Road - N34 47' 44.70, W118 51' 01.80"

Notes:

The Butterfield Route, through this segment, tracks the 1854 Banning Stage Route out of Antelope Valey into the Bear Valley and further into Grapevine Valley.

The location of Reed's Ranch can be placed with some certainty according to extrapolations from several historical resources and local research.

"Reed's Ranch" was located in the present-day community of Gorman, California.

The Conklings noted "… Reed's at Gorman, the next station fourteen miles west of French John's. Reed's ranch house and station was located at the foot of the hills on the south side of the road in what is now Gorman. Reed built a substantial one-story-and-a-half log house on this location which became the Butterfield station in 1858. This building was standing in a well pre-served state until in the summer of 1933, when it was razed. It is a matter of regret that this old building, the only log built station standing on the route in California, has not been preserved."

The fact that this area is on the San Andreas Fault and was near the epicenter of one of the worst earthquakes in California history actually helps us locate Reed's Ranch. That earthquake occurred along the San Andreas Fault on January 9, 1857, and is estimated to have measured 8.0 on the Richter scale.

According to local historian Bonnie Ketterl Kane:

In January 1857 the strongest earthquake to ever hit California centered in the nearby Tejon Pass. It was recorded that a woman died at Reed's Rancho when the beams of the house fell on her. Reed's Rancho was also listed on early maps as a road stop in the future area of Gorman.

A contemporaneous account of the earthquake in the *Santa Barbara Gazette* (January 22, 1857) reports that 'At Reed's Rancho, six miles from Tejon on the Los Angeles trail, the wife of Mr. Reed's vaquero was killed. A beam fell in the house on her head, killing her instantly.'

The Southern California Earthquake Data Center notes:

As a result of the shaking, the current of the Kern River was turned upstream, and water ran four feet deep over its banks. The waters of Tulare Lake were thrown upon its shores, stranding fish miles from the original lake bed. The waters of the Mokelumne River [east of Sacramento] were thrown upon its banks, reportedly leaving the bed dry in places. The Los Angeles River was reportedly flung out of its bed, too. Cracks appeared in the ground near San Bernardino and in the San Gabriel Valley. Some of the artesian wells in Santa Clara Valley ceased to flow, and others increased in output. New springs were formed near Santa Barbara and San Fernando. Ridges (moletracks) several meters wide and over a meter high were formed in several places. In Ventura, the mission sustained considerable damage, and part of the church tower collapsed. At Fort Tejon, where shaking was greatest, damage was severe. All around southern and central California, the strong shaking caused by the 1857 shock was reported to have lasted for at least one minute, possibly two or three!

The surface rupture caused by the quake was extensive. The San Andreas Fault broke the surface continuously for at least 350 km (220 miles), possibly as much as 400 km (250 miles), with an average slip of 4.5 meters (15 feet), and a maximum displacement of about 9 meters (30 feet) (possibly greater) in the Carrizo Plain area. Kerry Sieh (1978) noted that the Elkhorn Thrust, a low-angle thrust fault near the San Andreas, may have slipped simultaneously in the 1857 quake -- an observation that a team of researchers (1996) have recently used to support the idea that future movements along the San Andreas fault zone might produce simultaneous rupture on thrust faults in and near the Los Angeles area, causing a terrible 'double earthquake.'

On a less somber note, Kane notes of the Gorman area in general:

The settlement of Gorman has the unique honor of being one of the oldest continuously used roadside rest stops in California. The native people, traveling along their ancient trail system, would have stopped there when it was the Tataviam village of Kulshra'jek. By the early 1700s the Spanish had been using the native trail for some time and in the 1770s Capt. Pedro Fages wrote of passing the village as he traveled the road then called El Camino Viejo — The Old Way. The first *Americanos* in Alta California also followed the Spanish in stopping to rest and feed their horses in the beautiful mountain meadows and streams that surrounded the village now known as Gorman.

Between the gold rush of the late 1840s and early 1850s, the founding of the Indian reservation at the bottom of Grapevine Canyon in 1851, and the founding of Fort Tejon at the top of Grapevine Canyon in 1854, the area of the future Gorman quickly became a popular stop for the freighters and travelers of the day.

Extrapolating the mileages from French John's Station and the citations of the further known Butterfield Station at Fort Tejon would place Reed's Ranch on Gorman Post Road in the vicinity of coordinates N34° 47' 48.88", W118° 51' 28.31".

During telephone interviews in March of 2010,however, local researchers Bonnie Ketterl Kane and Harrison Irving Scott both identified the known location of Reed's Ranch as "just southeast of the Carl's Jr. Restaurant" (which is at 49669 Gorman Post Road in Gorman - coordinates N34° 47' 44.70, W118° 51' 01.80").In correspondence as of January, 2012, researcher Fred Yeck confirmed the placement of Reed's Ranch at co-ordinates N34° 47' 44.70, W118° 51' 01.80", which essentially concurs with the position stated by Kane and Scott.

Ormsby does not specifically mention Reed's Ranch. Bailey identifies it as a mileage point in his report to Postmaster General Brown.

References:

Bailey, Goddard; *California -- Arrival of the Overland Mail -- Itinerary of the Route*; as reported by newspaper article; *New York Times* (NY) - October 14, 1858.

Bailey, Goddard; *Report to Postmaster General A.V. Brown - Full itinerary as reported by De Bow's Review and Industrial Resources, Statistics etc;* published by De Bow's Review; New Orleans and Washington City; 1858. See specifically *Internal Improvements - 1. Wagon Road to the Pacific;* pp 719-721. Internet accessible at http://books.google.com/books?id=5CYoAAAAYAAJ&pg=PA720&lpg=PA720&dq=Cienega+de+los+Pimas&source=bl&ots=_5lZw_Bq23&sig=T6scCb8cpbY7KwjxpYoNvZpcgvI&hl=en&ei=i6KnS6KNOIr2M5yprIED&sa=X&oi=book_result&ct=result&resnum=2&ved=_0CAwQ6AEwAQ#v=onepage&q=Cienega%20de%20los%20Pimas&f=false (accessed March 22, 2010).

Conkling, Roscoe P. and Margaret B.; *The Butterfield Overland Mail, 1857–1869* (3 vols.); Glendale, CA: A. H. Clark Company, 1947.

Kane, Bonnie Ketterl; *A History of Gorman*; Santa Clarita Valley Historical Society; internet publication; http://www.scvhistory.com/scvhistory/kane-gorman-2002.htm (accessed March 9, 2010).

Kielbasa, John R.; *Historic Adobes of Los Angeles County*; Dorrance Publishing Co; Pittsburgh (July 1998); Internet publication (partial) Things to Do in Los Angeles; http://www.laokay.com/halac/ (accessed March 9, 2010).

Ormsby, Waterman L.; *The Butterfield Overland Mail (Only Through Passenger on the First Westbound Stage)*; original publications *New York Herald* (NY) Sep 26 - Nov 19, 1858; republished by Henry E. Huntington Library and Art Gallery, San Marino CA, 1942 - 1998.

Scott, Harrison Irving; *Ridge Route - the Road That United California,* published by the author; Torrance CA; 2002.

Southern California Earthquake Data Center; *Fort Tejon Earthquake*; Internet publication at http://www.data.scec.org/chrono_index/forttejo.html (accessed June 6, 2010).

Yeck, Fred; *The Butterfield Overland Mail*; 2011 – unpublished monograph supplied by the author.

**Vicinity of Reed's Ranch, Gorman CA
(N34.796, W118.853).
Photo by Fred Yeck (2008).**

Reed's Ranch to Fort Tejon

January 5, 2011

Reed's Ranch - Gorman • Los Angeles County (N34° 47' 48.88", W118° 51' 28.31")

TO Fort Tejon - Fort Tejon State Historic Park • Kern County (N34° 52' 14.63", W118° 53' 57.73")

Approximate Actual Route Reed's Ranch to Fort Tejon

8.6 miles.

(1858 Bailey itinerary says 8 miles)

Notes:

The Butterfield Route from Reed's Ranch to Fort Tejon continues along a northwestward heading on the 1854 route established by Banning. Essentially following the modern course of Interstate 5 / Golden State Freeway, the actual Butterfield Route appears to have tracked along an earlier road through the valley – what is now known variously as Gorman Post Road, Peaceful Valley Road and Lebec Road. That route is also referred to as the "Old Ridge Route."

The Fort Tejon Station location is now within the Fort Tejon State Historic Park.

Fort Tejon State Historic Park is administered and operated by the California State Parks Department. There are a number of restored buildings located within the park but it is unclear whether the actual Butterfield station is among them.

According to information from the California State Parks department:

> "In August 1854, Major J.L. Donaldson, a quartermaster officer, chose the present site in Cañada de las Uvas. The site was handsome and promised adequate wood and water. It was just 17 miles southwest of the Sebastian Indian Reservation, and it was right on what Major Donaldson was convinced would become the main route between the Central valley and Southern California.

> For almost ten years, Fort Tejon was the center of activity in the region between Stockton and Los Angeles. The soldiers, known as Dragoons, garrisoned at Fort Tejon patrolled most of central and southern California and sometimes as far as Utah. Dragoons from Fort Tejon provided protection and policed the settlers, travelers and Indians in the region. People from all over the area looked to Fort Tejon for employment, safety, social activities and the latest news from back east."

The Fort Tejon Historical Association, an historical research and Civil War reenactment group, says of the fort:

> "Fort Tejon was founded in 1854 on Grapevine Creek, 17 miles from its originally intended location on Tejon Creek. Maj. Donaldson of the 1st U.S. Dragoons selected the site for the new Fort at its present location because of the ready availability of

water, fuel and forage. Originally called Camp Cañada de las Uvas for the wild grapes in the area, it was officially christened Fort Tejon, (Tejon meaning Badger in Spanish), over the objection of Brevet Lt. Col. Benjamin L. Beall, 1st Dragoons, who suggested "Fort Le Beck," after a trapper who had been killed by a bear there.

The primary purpose of the garrison at Fort Tejon was to protect and control the Indians on the Sebastian Indian Reservation, and to control the major north-south road through Grapevine Canyon. Fort Tejon was garrisoned by various companies of the 1st Dragoons, and briefly from late 1857 to 1858 by a detachment of the 3rd Artillery, serving as infantry. In December, 1856, the regimental headquarters of the 1st Dragoons was moved from Fort Union, New Mexico Territory, to Fort Tejon, where it remained until the post was abandoned on June 15, 1861.

The rapidly expanding war in the eastern United States forced the government to recall the Army to the new seat of hostilities as fast as possible. This need for troops back in the East along with a growing fear of pro-secessionist activities in the Los Angeles and San Bernardino areas, ultimately forced the closure of Fort Tejon."

As to the Butterfield station specifically, William Tallack, an English diarist and Butterfield passenger, noted in his diary for June 14, 1860:

"Near midnight our conductor called out, 'Straighten yourselves up!' in preparation for some very rough ground that we were just approaching which had been broken by fissures and banks, caused by an earthquake. In about an hour after these arousing jolts we drew up at the foot of the Tejon Pass.

The Tejon station was a store kept by a dry sort of Yankee, who, after moving about very leisurely, and scarcely deigning to answer any questions put him, set before us a supper of goat's flesh and coffee. After making a hearty meal we had again to shift into another vehicle similar to the preceding."

Tallack's Butterfield writings have been transcribed in W.B. Lang's 1940 book *The First Overland Mail, Butterfield Trail, St. Louis to San Francisco, 1858-1861.*

Lang's *First Overland Mail, Butterfield Trail, St. Louis to San Francisco, 1858-1861* and the companion volume *First Overland Mail, Butterfield Trail, San Francisco to Memphis, 1858-1861* also contain several other transcriptions of Butterfield travel diaries, period letters-to-the-editor and contemporary correspondent reports on the route and stations as published in the *Daily Alta California,* and other California newspapers in 1858.

While not as detailed as the Ormsby and Bailey reports, these transcriptions as published by Lang are still helpful as supporting documents for the route and station locations.

Lang also includes transcriptions of the Ormsby reports for the *New York Herald* as well as Bailey's full written report to Postmaster General Brown as was also published in *De Bow's Review* (1858).

Ormsby states quite clearly that the Fort Tejon Station "... is directly in the pass and has some very fine adobe buildings, most of which belong to the government. There are few settlers."

That description would appear to place the actual along Lebec Road slightly east of the entrance to the Fort Tejon State Historic Park.

The California Historical Sites Marker at the Historic Park (#129 Fort Tejon notes "This military post was established by the United States Army on June 24, 1854, to suppress stock rustling and protect the Indians in the San Joaquin Valley. Camels for transportation were introduced here in 1858. As regimental headquarters of the First Dragoons, Fort Tejón was an important military, social, and political center - it was abandoned September 11, 1864."

William G. Hample's *Historical Site Markers - Kern County* confirms the location of this historical marker as being "Fort Tejon State Historic Park, on Lebec Road, 2.8 miles north of Lebec." Hample also includes a photo of the marker by Robert E. Crabtree.

Ormsby and Bailey both specifically mention Fort Tejon. Hoover discusses the historical importance in some depth, as do Pittman and Scott.

References:

Bailey, Goddard; *California -- Arrival of the Overland Mail -- Itinerary of the Route*; as reported by newspaper article; New York Times (NY) - October 14, 1858

Bailey, Goddard; *Report to Postmaster General A.V. Brown - Full itinerary as reported by De Bow's Review and Industrial Resources, Statistics etc*; published by De Bow's Review; New Orleans and Washington City; 1858. See specifically *Internal Improvements - 1. Wagon Road to the Pacific*; pp 719-721. Internet accessible at
http://books.google.com/books?id=5CYoAAAAYAAJ&pg=PA720&lpg=PA720&dq=Cienega+de+los+Pimas&source=bl&ots=_5lZw_Bq23&sig=T6scCb8cpbY7K wjxpYoNvZpcgvI&hl=en&ei=i6KnS6KNOIr2M5yprIED&sa=X&oi=book_result& ct=result&resnum=2&ved=_0CAwQ6AEwAQ#v=onepage&q=Cienega%20de% 20los%20Pimas&f=false (accessed March 22, 2010)

California State Parks; *Fort Tejon - About the Fort*; Internet publication at http://www.parks.ca.gov/?page_id=1165 (accessed June 6, 2010)

California State Parks - Office of Historic Preservation; California Historical Landmarks; Internet database -
http://www.parks.ca.gov/default.asp?page_id=21387 (accessed April 4, 2010)

Conkling, Roscoe P. and Margaret B.; *The Butterfield Overland Mail, 1857–1869* (3 vols); Glendale, CA: A. H.   Clark Company, 1947

Fort Tejon Historical Association; *History of Fort Tejon*; Internet publication accessible at http://www.forttejon.org/ (accesed June 6, 2010)

Hample, William G.; *Historical Site Markers - Kern County*; Kern County Historical Society; Bakersfield CA; 1991

Hoover, Mildred Brooke, Hero Eugene Rensch and Ethel Grace Rensch; *Historic Spots in California*; Stanford University Press; Stanford CA; 1932 (rev 1948)

Lang, W. B. (Editor); *The First Overland Mail, Butterfield Trail St. Louis to San Francisco, 1858-1861* and *The First Overland Mail, Butterfield Trail, San Francisco to Memphis, 1858-1861*; East Aurora, New York; 1945

Ormsby, Waterman L.; *The Butterfield Overland Mail (Only Through Passenger on the First Westbound Stage)*; original publications New York

Herald (NY) Sep 26 - Nov 19, 1858; republished by Henry E. Huntington Library and Art Gallery, San Marino CA, 1942 - 1998.

Pittman, Ruth; *Roadside History of California*; Mountain Press Publishing; Missoula MT; 1995

Scott, Harrison Irving; *Ridge Route - The Road That United California*, published by the author; Torrance CA; 2002

**Preserved building at Fort Tejon Historic Site
(N34.874, W118.895).
Photo by Fred Yeck (2008).**

148

ABOUT THE AUTHOR

Kirby Sanders is a career journalist, writer and historical researcher originally from Houston, Texas, and presently living in Northwest Arkansas. His writing endeavors have included poetry, short fiction, journalism and historical research reports.

During the late 1960s through the 1980s, he was active in the Southern Seed Poets Guild and Poets' Workshop literary groups in Houston. During that time he published several collections of poetry and edited several small literary journals. He also assisted in literary projects with Wings Press of Houston.

Among his early writing credits was publication in *From Hide and Horn, A Sesquicentennial Anthology of Texas Poets* published by Eakin Press of Austin, Texas, in 1986 wherein 150 Texas writers were selected to write a work encapsulating one year in Texas history.

In the early 1970s, he was employed as a writer and reporter with the *Houston (TX) Chronicle*. During the 1980s, he branched out into travel and tourism writing. During the 1990s he returned to daily journalism and worked at newspapers in East Texas and Northwest Arkansas.

During that time, he received several awards for investigative reporting. Amongst those was a substantial series on the arrest of the final suspect in the 1963 Sixteenth Street Baptist Church bombing in Birmingham, Alabama -- the infamous "Four Little Girls" murder case.

Many of his feature stories during that time focused on the history of the communities in which he worked. He has also worked in film, radio and television.

In 2011, he was selected as a consultant to the National Park Service to prepare a substantial report and mapping survey on the 1858-1861 Butterfield Overland Mail stagecoach route in the states of Missouri, Arkansas, Oklahoma, Texas, New Mexico, Arizona and California.

He has also authored two novels, *A Death In Texas* and *Nusquam Res, Nusquam Esse; the Final Journey of Ambrose Bierce*.